children's rooms

children's rooms

PRACTICAL DESIGN SOLUTIONS
FOR AGES 0–10

Joanna Copestick

For Hannah and Julia and their cousins and
second cousins, 25 of them at the last count.
And godson Magnus.

First published in 2002 by
Conran Octopus Limited
A part of Octopus Publishing Group
2–4 Heron Quays
London E14 4JP
www.conran-octopus.co.uk

Reprinted in 2003
Paperback edition published in 2005
ISBN 1 84091 457 2

Text © Joanna Copestick 2002
Design and layout © Conran
Octopus 2002
Illustration © Conran Octopus 2002

Printed and bound in China

British Library Cataloguing-in-
Publication Data
A catalogue record for this book is
available from the British Library

Publishing Director: Lorraine Dickey

Senior Editor: Muna Reyal

Managing Editor: Helen Ridge

Creative Director: Leslie Harrington

Art Editor: Alison Fenton

Picture Research: Rachel Davies

Photography for case studies: Winfried Heinze

Photography for projects: Verity Welstead

Stylist for special photography: Cathy Sinker

Illustrator: Russell Bell

Senior Production Controller: Manjit Sihra

introduction

One of the many exciting aspects of becoming a parent is the thought of planning and decorating a nursery for your baby. And once you become a parent and adapt your life to the rigours of caring for a new member of the family, you will soon start to think about how to transform the nursery into a room suitable for an older child. Whatever your personal style, this definitive guide will help you plan your child's room from the day your baby is born right up to the age of ten.

A nursery is relatively easy to plan because a baby's needs are simple and straightforward, but a child's room is more than just somewhere to sleep: it is also a place for relaxation, solitude and play. Children usually like to be closely involved in deciding how their rooms will look, expressing strong opinions on such topics as paint colours, wall treatments and soft furnishings. And, increasingly, parents are taking notice of them, furnishing and decorating the rooms in such a way that their children feel at home in their own space, but without compromising on taste.

Children's rooms are often among the smallest in the house, so maximizing the available space is important. In this book, there are ideas and information on layout and decorating, storage, safety and soft furnishings, organic living and outdoor rooms. Practical projects will inspire you to create your own solutions for different aspects of your child's room and earn you top parenting marks from your offspring.

To complement it all, there are case studies of the homes of real families who have devised ingenious solutions to the challenge of living in style with their children.

planning

THE IMPORTANCE OF PLANNING

The best children's spaces are colourful and inviting, busy but tidy, lively yet calming. They are achieved only with advance planning, which allows you to think about your favourite decorative style and design the space so that there's enough storage, plenty of visual interest and a cosy sleeping area.

Starting a family is a significant stage in your life. Once your baby is born, you switch from a relatively carefree existence to a more structured, considered routine – if only for the sake of your own sanity. The effect that a new baby has on your home is a similarly life-altering event. One minute you may have a spare room, albeit crammed with shelves of things you've been meaning to sort out for ages, but extraneous space, nevertheless. The next minute you have to fit a newborn baby, a cot (crib), some storage, seating and a play area into the very same room. Suddenly the space you had taken for granted feels a lot smaller and, in time, so does your home. But careful planning can mean the difference between a hastily compiled mix of disparate elements and a cohesive scheme that has the capacity for flexibility, renewable interest and practicality for years to come.

PAST AND PRESENT

The Victorians expected children to be 'seen and not heard', and it was commonplace for their rooms to be tiny, often far away from their parents under the eaves and out of earshot. As time went on, children's rooms began to develop as part of the home rather than as an afterthought. Toys and sometimes small-scale furniture for seating and storage were introduced into them. However, they were still a long way from the havens of comparative indulgence that we create for our children today.

Children's rooms have assumed a new importance in the home. These days, 'pester power' is an acknowledged marketing tool and is used shamelessly by advertisers to hustle busy and distracted parents into appeasing their demanding offspring with the latest toy or gadget. The disintegration of the traditional nuclear family, coupled with an increasing reliance on technology to replace family interaction, has meant that a child's own personal space plays a more significant role.

Bear in mind that children grow and develop at a rate that tends to outstrip their parents' ability to keep up. Just when you thought you'd cracked the perfect nursery, your toddler starts to walk and decides that low-level decorative borders need peeling off. And when you've finally got around to framing your pre-schooler's paintings and hanging them on the wall, she brings home an even better work of art that needs instant wall space. Enjoy these years, because soon

your nine-year-old will be appealing for permission to stick torn-out pictures of cuddly animals or pubescent pop stars on the walls with gungy adhesives that leave greasy marks behind them.

Keep a constant eye on the future and remember to anticipate the next stage in your child's development. Don't be fooled into thinking that your children won't want to move on to a new look every few years.

By involving your children in planning a particular aspect of their own room, you will encourage their creativity, but make sure that they know it's you who makes the ultimate decisions. While they may complain about restrictions, they will actually enjoy the fact that you're allowing them to contribute their ideas without having to take on the responsibility of making the 'right' choices. You can also feel free to remind them that they chose the wall colour when, a year later, they grumble that their room is not looking as cool as those of their four or five closest friends!

LEFT Children do not necessarily require vast expanses of decorated walls. Sometimes a panel of strong colour is enough to punctuate a space and provide definition in a junior room.

FAR LEFT Attic rooms are often a popular space for adapting as children's rooms. This one, despite being an awkward space, is perfect for twin cots and roomy enough to transform into a shared toddlers' bedroom later on.

THE NURSERY

Creating a room for your first child is part of the fun and wonder of starting a family, and it can sometimes seem every bit as daunting. But then again it does give you the chance to indulge in whatever decorative style you favour: whimsy, restraint, colour or calm. Whatever design style you choose, it's important to plan the space before you begin the fun part of choosing colours and motifs because good planning should mean getting it right first time.

One of the main considerations to bear in mind is that babies change and develop at a rapid rate. You may find that your primary painted furniture or painstakingly applied nursery stencils start to date well before they wear out, so keep hold of the notion that constant change and flexibility are inevitable in anything to do with offspring.

Remember that your child may occupy this one room for the first few years of life, so think ahead if you want to avoid redecorating every year. Choose colours with care and avoid too many purely babyish elements that will date quickly. You can then use accessories to create a nursery atmosphere, as they are easy and inexpensive to change later.

It's tempting to rush out and buy everything new for your first child, but you can often make do with second-hand items, especially those that won't see much use. Wooden cribs, chairs brought up to date with new upholstery or slip covers and battered chests of drawers stripped and repainted all make great nursery furniture, and some of them can probably be re-used elsewhere in the house at a later date.

Creating your own heirlooms is also easy at this stage. Invest in a painted toy chest, a small desk and chair or a set of shelves and a collection of nursery books that can be passed through the family from one generation to the next.

RIGHT Freestanding cupboards provide useful storage for all ages. They can be repainted to match the changing decor as the child grows older, and will hide anything from nappies (diapers) and toiletries now to board games and clothes later on.

Once you have allocated a room or space to your baby, you can plan the layout. If you're remodelling as well as redecorating, take the opportunity to consider heating, lighting and storage needs. Replace old, unreliable radiators with a smaller, contemporary version. Babies' rooms need to be a consistent temperature for the first few months (see page 25), so if the baby is born during the winter, check that your heating system is in good working order.

ABOVE Making a feature of the cot means that you can shift the focus to a bed later on. A fabric canopy encloses the sleeping space and will not be wasted on a toddler or older child either.

SITING A NURSERY

For the first couple of months you may find that your baby sleeps in your bedroom. If you are breastfeeding or have had a Caesarean delivery, it is much easier to have your baby sleep next to your bed in a Moses basket, so that you don't have to move too far in the middle of the night.

A spare room, which is often the smallest bedroom, can be decorated as a nursery. If you don't have a spare room but a large bedroom, consider turning one room into two and create a nursery that way. Ideally, for at least the first year or so, the nursery should be on the same level as your bedroom and as close to it as possible for easy access.

Babies require only the basics for a comfortable life, so keep it simple. Even a tiny spare room provides adequate space for a child up to the age of two, as long as there is room for a cot or cot bed with perhaps a mobile hanging over it, a small chest of drawers and a bedside light.

If your nursery has to be crammed into a really small space, make good use of the walls for storage. During the first year, your storage needs may be met by peg rails fixed to the wall and a freestanding cupboard or chest of drawers, while a toy basket or two should be enough to swoop up a growing collection of squeaky animals and noisy rattles.

If the ceiling is high, use the space above door height for shelving or suspend baskets from the ceiling. Use other rooms for storing little-used items, and consider knocking through to an adjacent room to enlarge the space. (See also the chapter on storage, pages 58–91.)

LEFT A squeaky clean, all-white nursery exudes a natural calm and pleasing simplicity. Painted floors are both appealing and anti-allergy, while a sheepskin rug provides a soft surface underfoot.

NURSERY LIGHTING

Lighting is very important in a nursery. In the early months, when nighttime feeding is a regular ritual, you will need a subtle nightlight – bright enough for you to see what you're doing, but also sufficiently dim so that your baby does not become too wakeful and alert. This soft lighting will also prove useful when you pop into the nursery to check that your baby is fast asleep. A dimmable overhead pendant light is ideal for this, but a low-wattage table lamp would also work well, provided that it has a stable base. A small nightlight placed in an electrical socket or close to the cot is a useful device. This is also a handy place for plugging in the baby alarm.

Wherever the nursery is, make sure that there's dimmable lighting en route from your bedroom, so you can see your way there without having to turn on bright overhead lights in the middle of the night. If the nursery is in an attic or down another flight of stairs, you could light the route with round halogen lights set into the wall above every other step, nautical style. This looks neat and is highly practical, too, as it will help prevent everyone from tripping over discarded toys when the children are older.

Babies love bright colours so you could install some fairy lights along one wall and switch them on occasionally for visual interest. Always keep them out of reach and well away from the cot area, though. Brightly coloured lampshades are relatively inexpensive and can be swapped about for variety. Rectangular 3-D nursery lights that project small images of stars and teddies around the walls will also provide great entertainment for young eyes.

RIGHT In this classically inspired nursery, a string of paper lanterns gives a warming glow to bedtime. Always make sure that they're placed well out of reach of babies.

FLOORING

Comfort is so closely associated with babyhood that it's very tempting to rush out and buy a soft, luxurious carpet for a new nursery. Bear in mind, though, that your helpless baby will, in the space of a year, become an adept spiller of drinks, cookies and any form of lotion found within arm's reach. Maybe the wall-to-wall fashionable shag pile can wait until the next revival and you can make do with ordinary, economy carpet for a while. You may even be better off with stripped and painted or stained floorboards or a laminate floor, softened with a generous rug that nearly covers the room (add an anti-slip mat underneath). Alternatively, go for a minimal look and choose a hardwearing rubber, linoleum or vinyl floor.

Natural matting may be organic in spirit and fairly kind to allergy sufferers but it's rough on babies when they start to crawl. If allergies and asthma run in the family, remember that carpet is a great attracter of dust and dust mites, so the hard floor and rug option is probably a safer choice.

WINDOWS

The most important thing about window treatments in nurseries is that they include a black-out lining, especially in the summer months. Once your baby has established a sleeping routine the last thing you want is for her to wake up at dawn when light starts to leak into the room. If you make the black-out lining detachable, it can be added to existing curtains or blinds (shades) and perhaps removed during the winter, although it does also provide insulation. Roman and roller blinds work well and, kept plain, can be made more interesting with a decorative wooden or fabric pelmet. Once again, it's tempting to go mad for nursery-inspired fabrics, but think about using them sparingly, such as on tiebacks and cushions.

RIGHT A chequerboard design is timeless, ageless and suitable for children of either gender. Here it is painted as a panel in the centre of a nursery floor, but it could be extended over the whole floor. It could also be embellished with a defining or decorative border around the edge of the room.

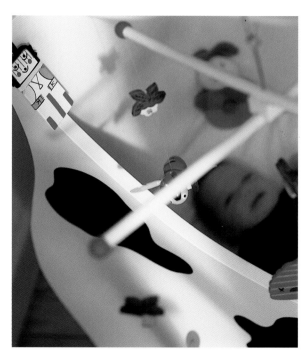

LEFT A painted cot becomes an instant heirloom, particularly if it has been decorated by someone in the family or specially commissioned as a one-off. Protect it with a coat of water-based, preferably organic, matt varnish. A mobile hung above the cot, out of reach but close enough to be seen easily, will provide a good source of entertainment.

FURNITURE

Choose your initial furniture for the nursery with care and allow the rest of the room to develop with time. Think about how many years your child may use this room for sleeping. If you envisage moving house after a while, don't go overboard creating a nursery that Peter Pan would be proud of. Save your energy for enjoying your pregnancy.

CHOOSING A COT

The cot (crib) is the single most important piece of furniture in your child's first room, so make sure that you choose one that will last if you are planning to have a large family. Comfort should be top of the list of priorities but also think about your personal style and choose one that most closely fits your decorating ethos. Deciding which one to buy is not as straightforward as it looks – you can choose from a plain wood or painted one, rocking or stable, a cot bed or an adjustable base-height model, low-level, with or without integral playbeads, and so on.

RIGHT Cots that are fitted with adjustable-height bases are versatile pieces of nursery furniture. At the highest position – suitable only before the baby becomes mobile – they are easy on parents' backs, while the lowest position allows the cot to be used for a longer time. Some will also convert to cot beds once your baby becomes a toddler. This painted version has deep slats, chunky feet and a plain wooden rail around the edge, offering a convenient resting place for small toys.

Vintage-style cots

Antique wooden cots create their own statement instantly and are perfectly safe to use, provided you buy a new mattress that fits well and bedding. The cot is often the one piece of nursery furniture that is preserved in the attic waiting for the next generation. If you need to strip and repaint a second-hand cot, remember that pregnant women should not inhale old paint fumes that might be laced with lead. Use low VOC-rated (volatile organic compound) water-based emulsion paint or, better still, organic paints (see pages 134–7). White-painted cots from the 1960s with stylized blue and pink animal motifs look distinctly vintage these days and are likely soon to become collectable items. French iron cots are perfectly charming, although not quite as safe as wooden cots as they tend to have larger gaps between their curving struts. Traditional wooden cribs are delightful and enduring heirlooms that can double up as dolls' beds when your child is older.

Contemporary cots

Oval-shaped varnished plywood cots offer contemporary curves, while a low-level mattress dropped into a white-painted slatted surround looks cool and modern in both the city and the country. It's always easiest to have a freestanding cot so that you can access it from any angle.

Cot beds are a good investment provided that they convert to a single bed of decent proportions and you are planning to have more than one child. Check before you buy because some beds are suitable for children only up to the age of three or four.

ABOVE This metal designer cot, inspired by traditional hospital beds, can be moved from one large, open-plan space to another – the ultimate in flexible sleeping arrangements.

ABOVE LEFT Cool babies require cool sleeping spaces. This ultra-contemporary day cot would suit any urban loft.

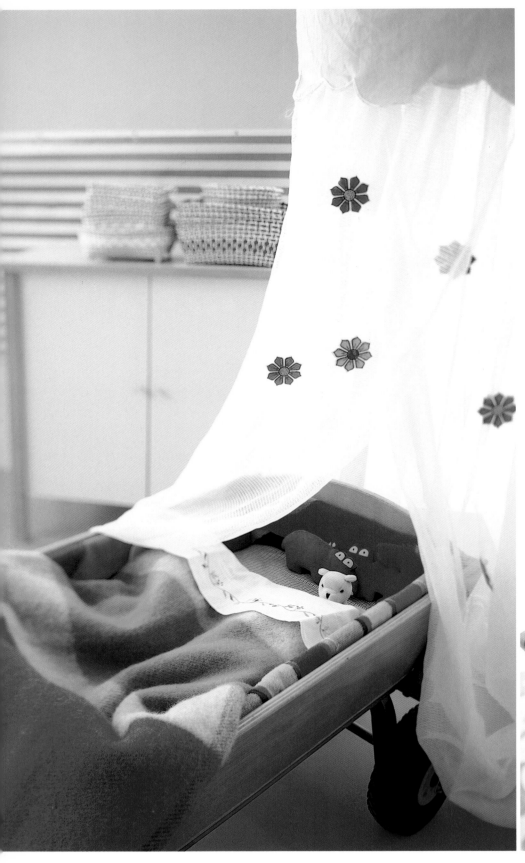

LEFT Sometimes the temptation to indulge in a novelty crib is just too great to resist. Comfort yourself with the knowledge that it will soon become a well-used plaything for older children.

BELOW A collapsible cot for a baby who is often on the move is even more appealing when made from animal-print fabric supported on a clean-lined wooden framework.

Moses baskets

These range from a traditional woven basket with handles and perhaps a collapsible hood to a fabric-covered carrycot that detaches from a pram or pushchair. Whichever you choose, it will be suitable only for approximately the first three months of your baby's life, so borrow, inherit or buy second-hand if you can, because they are useful to have in the early days. You are likely to need a stand to rest the basket on and these can be bought separately.

CHANGING TABLES

You will always need somewhere in the nursery where you can change nappies (diapers). The most basic arrangement is to place a changing mat on top of a small chest of drawers or, if you don't mind bending over, on the floor, which is safer once your baby starts wriggling around. There are many different types of

purpose-made changing tables on the market. Some are designed to convert into little tables later on, while others are simply small pieces of furniture that can be used for storage once the nappy stage has passed. Other tables have lockable castors so you can move them around – a particularly good idea if you live in an open-plan space.

Whatever you choose, make sure that you can use it comfortably and that it doesn't strain your back while you work. Find a changing surface that allows a little extra space around your baby. Fit a mobile or other

ABOVE Old furniture can double as a changing table that not only is practical but also looks good.

ABOVE LEFT Purpose-built changing tables are often considered a necessity for nurseries, but bear in mind that they have a limited lifespan. This beech bench could easily become a simple storage unit at a later date.

LEFT This charming changing table has been created from recycled timber and painted to blend in with the neutral walls and floor. Display shelves defined with a picture frame provide a movable showcase within easy reach.

source of visual interest near the table. As your baby enters the wriggling phase, give her a toy or book to distract her while you change the nappy. If you use a simple chest of drawers, you'll have storage space for clean nappies, a change of clothes, cotton wool (absorbent cotton) and wipes. If you also keep your changing bag here, you will avoid the frantic search for it every time you want to leave the house in a hurry.

SEATING

A comfortable chair for night feeding is important for mother and baby to keep cosy and, hopefully, sleepy. In the daytime, you will want a chair where you can sit and feed your baby or just flop while you watch her kick around on the changing table or play on the floor as she gets bigger. An adult-sized beanbag would do the same job in a contemporary setting.

SAFETY ISSUES

Make sure that there are no trailing flexes (electric cords) that you can trip over in the night. Once your baby is more mobile, move everything out of reach that is within grabbing distance of the cot. A rug laid on a wooden floor should have a slip-resistant mat underneath it, and avoid having slippery high-gloss paint on the bedroom floor during pregnancy or once your baby is born. Don't place the cot close to a radiator or draughty window, as your baby shouldn't have to work too hard regulating her own temperature. The recommended temperature range for the rooms of newborn babies is 19–22° C (66–72° F). A baby alarm will allow you to listen in when your baby is asleep and alert you when she is crying.

RIGHT A large, comfy armchair is a welcoming sight in a nursery, and an attractive slip cover makes it practical, too, as the cover can easily be removed for cleaning.

THE TODDLER'S ROOM

Your precious baby has turned into a small person who is always on the move and loves to explore and play, sometimes for short periods on her own, so her room should accommodate this sense of adventure and curiosity, while being safe for her to use. For the most part, she will still want to be close to her carer, but occasionally she will wander off and play alone in her own surroundings. Creating a toddler's bedroom calls for versatility and also an eye on the forthcoming school-age years.

Safety and a sensible layout are of paramount importance at this stage of a child's life. Toddlers are at their most inquisitive and fearless when they are least aware of dangers. As a quick safety test, get down on all fours in your toddler's room and see if you spot any hazards – trailing flexes, small toys that can be swallowed, and lotions and potions left lying around are all potential dangers for roaming toddlers. It's important to store any toys with small components well out of reach of your toddler, and make sure that bottles and medicines are also kept at a safe height.

For safety reasons, it's still a good idea to keep the bed away from the window and any radiators. A baby alarm close to the bed is still useful, particularly when your toddler takes daytime naps.

It's possible that a younger sibling is now on the scene, so you may have a baby and a small child sharing a room. In addition to the nursery basics, you will need to make sure that your older child feels at home, too, so make an effort to provide a few special elements just for her, such as soft toy storage, a bookcase, new bedlinen or a height chart.

RIGHT The main element of a toddler's room is the bed and this elegant traditional bed shows how useful cot beds can be, especially when they're chosen to fit into a well-proportioned, airy bedroom.

FURNITURE AND STORAGE

When your child is between the ages of two and two-and-a-half, you can dispense with the cot and install a bed. A cot bed will, of course, adapt into a suitable bed, but if you are having another baby, you may still want to continue using it as a cot.

When buying a new bed, there are several options to consider. With an eye on the future, you may want to buy a single bed that can be turned into a bunk bed later on when your family expands. If space is tight, then a built-in cabin bed with integral storage underneath is a neat solution.

Moving from a cot to a bed is a big step, so make it as exciting as possible by providing one that's fun, comfortable and inviting. Platform beds or bunks are not suitable for children this young, but painted headboards or novelty beds that look like boats, cars or princess bedsteads are just right. Canopies of wood, MDF (medium-density fibreboard) or fabric can be suspended from the ceiling for a fantasy element. Making a feature of the bed means that you can employ restraint in the rest of the room. If up until now your child has had a cot sheet and blankets or a cot duvet, you can move up to a full-size single duvet.

While useful only up to the age of six or so, miniature furniture, particularly small chairs and sofas, is invaluable in a toddler's room, as all children love to sit and copy adult behaviour. It is also useful for encouraging independent play. Customized or painted wooden chairs are always remembered into adulthood and fit into any kind of adult room when required. Children also love beanbags from an early age – as seats, playthings and, occasionally, as weapons! Built-in low-level seats can double as storage areas, and freestanding storage chests can double as seats with the addition of padding and fabric on their lids. A small desk and chair or beanbag placed close to low-level

shelves of books or toys mean that a child can become more independent and practise her motor skills. Just make sure that she's not 'practising' on trailing flexes, bottles of perfume or a make-up bag.

Storage requirements will start to expand as wardrobe space, books and larger toys begin to encroach on the room. A combination of built-in storage and freestanding pieces is the most flexible. You can still use some of the nursery furniture: the toy storage box and the comfy nursing chair, for example, and perhaps the nursery shelving, which you might choose to repaint.

ABOVE A low-level sleigh bed can be easily transformed into a miniature four-poster by adding and securing single bed posts. Drape them with a muslin canopy and individual decorations at each post.

Miniature furniture such as a table and chairs may seem like an indulgence but it is extremely useful. Children love being able to carry out tasks at their own level.

Child-size wardrobes are undeniably appealing but they do have a limited lifespan. Instead, look for vintage school lockers, old armoires or tallboys for instant style and personality. There is no need for a proper wardrobe or another form of tall clothes storage until your child is about seven years old. If you do have a wardrobe already, though, make the most of the space by putting a chest of drawers inside it, or adding shelves or another hanging rail lower down.

Ways of accommodating toys seamlessly into the room become a big priority for toddler spaces. Plastic crates of toy food, whirring electronic toys, push-along tricycles and miniature kitchens seem to have become necessities for the modern toddler. You can never have enough medium-sized containers for these, so if your built-in storage is crammed full, use freestanding

items to add to it. Big baskets, wooden boxes on castors and the trusty toy box all work wonders for a quick tidy-up. Keeping them at a low level means not only that your toddler can reach them safely, but also that you can train her in the art of mess-busting at an early age. Providing a place for everything helps her learn where to find things, too, and where to put them back later. (For more storage ideas, see pages 58–79.)

Toddlers are fickle and flighty creatures who quickly become familiar with their toys. If you can, preserve a space such as some pigeonhole shelves or a bookcase where you can display frequently used toys. Every couple of months, swap them around for others you have tucked away in the attic or garage. Your toddler will react to them as if they are a whole new set of playthings.

LEFT Miniature furniture in a child's room will give you more wall space on which to make a bold statement. Here, two walls devoted to a large-scale landscape are highly contemporary and a great way of enlivening an unremarkable room. Choose specialist wallpaper – the more realistic-looking the better – or create your own montage with enlarged colour photocopies or enormous posters. Simply remove the paper when their appeal dates.

LIGHTING

A lamp on a bedside table is a must for toddler bedtime reading. Novelty wall lights, such as cartoon characters, boats and so on, are an alternative if the room is small.

Check that your wall sockets are positioned in suitable places and that you have enough of them for bedside lights and appliances such as music systems for bedtime story tapes. Make sure that you position the sockets carefully so that there will be no trailing flexes for your toddler to trip over.

If you didn't have a dimmer switch while the room was used as a nursery, now's a good time to install one, as your child will still be taking daytime naps. Novelty lampshades can be matched to favourite themes. By now your child will no doubt be showing leanings for football, fairies, trucks or cartoon characters, and a light is a less indulgent and cheaper way of reacting to their preferences than concocting a whole new scheme for the room.

At this age, recessed ceiling lights are a good idea, as they reduce the need for freestanding table or standard lamps, which can so easily be knocked over. They also produce a good light for artistic activities such as drawing and painting.

FLOORING

Hardwearing bedroom flooring is vital at this stage in a child's development. The best solutions in this heavy-use area include stripped and painted, varnished or stained floorboards, softened with chunky woollen rugs

LEFT Retro floral blinds are decorative but discreet in a girl's bedroom, and are more likely to survive a few changes of wall colour than other, more ostentatious designs. Blinds tend to make more economic sense than curtains, and trimmings will add interest to plain blinds, especially if you involve your child in choosing them.

in bright colours to make a more welcoming surface. The floorboards will be easy to keep clean, but choose rugs that are washable. When stripping and sanding floorboards, make sure that you fill any larger gaps between boards to prevent small toys disappearing through them.

While carpets are the softest and most luxurious floorcovering to have in a child's room, they are not always the most practical or healthiest option. However, if you had floorboards in the nursery, you may want to lay a carpet now that your toddler is fully mobile, especially as children of this age like to sit or lie on the floor to play with toys. If you prefer the natural look, choose a carpet that resembles natural matting. The slightly textured finish will show fewer dirty marks than a plain carpet.

WINDOWS

Windows are another point of interest in a toddler's room. A plain roman blind in a bright colour may be decorated with fake flowers or with felt cars or animal shapes. Simple eyelet- or tab-headed curtains look good in a young child's room, particularly if the wooden curtain poles are painted to match or contrast with the walls and embellished with novelty pole ends. If you're splashing out on curtains for the first time, think about choosing a fairly timeless fabric. Trimmings such as buttons or fringing are a good way of making changes without breaking the bank; similarly, tie-backs are easier to update than whole curtains. Checks, stripes and ginghams appeal equally well to boys and girls, children and adults.

Fit safety catches to windows if you are at all concerned about your child being too inquisitive about the windowsill and what's going on outside. These will allow you to let in some fresh air without your child being able to open the window fully.

ABOVE Have fun with details in children's rooms. Decorate light switches with neoprene borders and add novelty light pulls to any lights operated by pull-cords to complete a scheme.

LEFT Walls and floors are as important as furniture when planning children's rooms. Simple shapes and patterns provide a sharp decorative focus in rooms where contemporary style matters. Small areas of wall colour work just as well as a room drenched in one colour. Floors may be decorated with patterned linoleum or vinyl or with modern paint stencils.

THE PRE-SCHOOLER'S ROOM

Between the ages of three and five, toddlers who were hitherto tantrum experts start to acquire the skills of sociable and civilized children – that's the theory, at least. All at once, the idea of being a mini-adult becomes irresistible and dressing-up starts to play a major part in their lives. Cowboys, princesses, cartoon superheroes, astronauts and simply mummies and daddies have constant appeal, so make sure that you set up some kind of dressing-up box or hanging rail in the bedroom. If you don't, it's more or less a foregone conclusion that they'll head straight for your wardrobe for a spot of 'let's pretend' with your neatly folded clothes and carefully arranged accessories.

These pre-school years are extremely precious. Children are naturally creative at this age and learn a great deal by experimenting with paint, materials and role-playing. Encourage them in their creativity by including the props they need in their room or, if there's not enough space, in a self-contained area elsewhere in the home.

Although pre-school children still prefer to play close to their parents or carers, they do gradually begin to entertain themselves alone or with friends for short periods in their own rooms. Make sure that the space is safe to be in and also provide some low-level storage to encourage their new-found independence and sense of adventure.

If the bedroom is to be shared by siblings, it can be fun to divide it subtly into areas. You could let each child have her own bedside rug for a subtle delineation of space, or join two low bookcases together to form a library or activity corner that divides the space in two. A height chart on the wall is another way of displaying two different identities, with each child choosing her own colour to mark her progress.

Boys are no different from girls when it comes to sibling rivalry over belongings. Matching beds look cute and prevent too many arguments about whose is better. You can equalize the scheme still further with bedside tables or with storage boxes or shelves at the end of each bed. Personalized table lamps and bedlinen are an effective way of allowing your children's individual personalities and interests to shine through any uniformity of furniture.

ABOVE Screens double as mobile puppet theatres and vital props for imaginative play, as well as being practical room dividers and versatile additions to any shared space.

MAKING CHANGES

The pre-school years are an important time for informal learning. Reinforce the alphabet and numbers by buying or making a rug that features the numbers one to ten or a small alphabet of capital and lower-case letters. It will help your child learn without her noticing. She will also be taking a great interest in books, both picture and reading, so make sure that the bedside lighting is adequate for the task. Encourage her to turn out her own light by fixing a wall-mounted light to the side of or above the bed, but buy only a child-safe version. At this age some children suffer badly from night terrors, so if your child has developed a fear of the dark, you could recycle the nursery nightlight and use the dimmer switch again.

The floor is a popular place for play and will regularly be covered with building bricks, dolls, train sets or other floor-based toys. If you have wall-to-wall carpet, have it treated with a proprietary stain-resistant chemical to preserve its life, or else lay a cheap, large rug over as big an area as possible for these years of heavy-duty wear. Floorboards, laminate floors, linoleum and tough vinyl are still the most forgiving of surfaces for this age. You can prevent possible accidents on slippery wood or laminate floors by putting down rugs with anti-slip mats underneath.

This is the time to acquire a full-sized single bed, so think carefully about the style you choose and whether you are likely to have any more children in the future. Single beds that convert to bunks later on are a good investment, as are bed units with storage underneath. Matching beds, perhaps with complementary bedlinen, look good in a shared room, dormitory style.

Create extra storage by placing a toy chest at the end of the bed. In a shared room two bedside tables and a cupboard or set of shelves each prevents arguments over territory and belongings.

ABOVE Personalized coat hooks encourage children to remember that their pyjamas and dressing gowns have a home. Paint or stain and stencil individual plaques and get the children to help.

You can encourage independence in your child by storing the clothes that she will be wearing the next day in an easily accessible place. Gradually she will start dressing herself in an ever-more convincing and appropriate manner, though be prepared for some unusual and startling combinations once she starts making her own choices.

Playtime is hugely important to this age group and a few pieces of furniture that double up as playthings are certain to be well used. A freestanding easel allows painting sessions to be self-contained, and it is easy to move to other parts of the house. Role-play, in the form of shopping, cooking and making things is particularly popular now. If you have the space, make a toy kitchen (see pages 148–9), cardboard puppet theatre or castle, any of which are guaranteed to be well used and loved.

LEFT A place for drawing and colouring is always welcome, so use the windowsill above a desk for keeping colouring materials tidy.

FAR LEFT In a tight space, a scaled-down bed can be purpose-built to fit the room. This platform bed, painted the same colour as the walls, allows the area beneath to be used for play and storage.

ABOVE Miniature kitchens are essential for small people, who never tire of imitating adults. They often create elaborate dinner parties with a minimum of plastic food and miniature cooking equipment. It is the one pre-school plaything that seems to appeal equally to boys and girls.

THE OLDER CHILD'S ROOM

Once your child starts school, you can no longer lay claim to being the most important part of her daily life. Her increasing independence may lead you to think that you're 'losing' your child, but in fact this age stage is a fine one, spanning the years of sweet childhood to the onset of pre-teen awareness. Indeed, many parents think it the optimum time of enjoyment for both themselves and their children. At the age of six, your child will still relish your company, so make the most of it because, by the age of ten, you will get glimpses of what kind of teenager she may turn into!

From the age of seven to ten, children undergo a transformation that becomes more and more marked. Often referred to as 'tweenagers', these young kids on the block are the embodiment of mini-teenagers. Although extremely sophisticated in many of their tastes, they are still in a lot of ways less 'streetwise' than previous generations of children who, after school, at weekends and during the school holidays, were allowed out to play in the street or the fields and only came home for tea.

Children in this age group become increasingly independent and like to spend time alone in their rooms. They really enjoy being involved in design decisions about the decor of their rooms, and they also like to help out with easy decorating tasks. Thanks to the explosion of interior design television programmes, magazines and books that has occurred over the last decade or so, they also have definite opinions about colour, layout and style. In addition, new technology in the form of computer games and educational software offers children the chance to see for themselves 3-D images of rooms and furniture layouts, raising their awareness of design to levels unheard of a generation ago.

LEFT Impose order on an older boy's room and the sports kit may one day be as neat as the trophies on display. Metal lockers are a smart way of making a room look ultra-cool as well as tidy. Metal bed frames are really popular with this age group as the wooden bed of early childhood is discarded in favour of a more sophisticated look.

OPPOSITE The pre-teen years of seven to eleven are different now from how they used to be. Girls are highly aware of fashion and appearance, not just in how they themselves look, but also in how their rooms look. Keep it simple, cool and funky, and don't forget the beanbag.

ADAPTING AND UPDATING

With school comes a whole new set of influences for your child. One day she's playing happily with a few dolls or a couple of building blocks, the next she may be demanding her room is painted bright orange with a border of hand-stencilled white daisies, just like the room of her best friend for that week. And so starts a period of negotiation and persuasion, but always remember who's boss. Children of this age are impatient beings; they like instant results yet remain fickle when it comes to sustained interest in living with favourite colours and styles.

The main room changes that are needed for this age group are finding a place for doing homework, accommodating growing quantities of books, games, clothes and technology and making space for friends to sleep over, although some children start enjoying these as young as five or six. Sleepovers have become such a routine part of life that a sleeping bag and an easily accessible overnight kit are essential parts of a seven- to nine-year-old's belongings. As long as there is some floor space, sleepovers are perfectly possible with a layer of spare duvets strewn across the room and a conglomeration of sleeping bags, futons, beanbags and pillows on top.

This is the age when girls and boys seem to separate out into Us and Them for a while, shunning each other's company in and out of school. Pet animals, however, do not receive the same disdain. If you're not a cat lover or dog lover or are allergic to both, be prepared to make bedroom space for a hamster cage or other small, low-maintenance pets

LEFT There is nothing as cool as a one-off feature to impress your friends. Visitors are no doubt in plentiful supply for this bedroom where swinging from the curtains takes on a whole new meaning. A mattress on the floor softens any falls and is also useful for sleepovers.

such as exotic lizards and slow-worms. If these all
sound too much like hard work, there's always the
goldfish option.

Shared spaces now need to be more definitely
defined areas. Rather than dividing the space into
territories, you could create a workstation where both
children can get on with their homework, a play area
they can share, plus a wardrobe or clothes rail and a
chest of drawers common to them both.

Storage needs to be thought through from a new
angle, and the decoration may need redoing, probably
with the help of your child and often incorporating her
most creative suggestions. If the bedroom is quite
small, now is a good time to set up a computer
workstation elsewhere in the house for the older
children. A kitchen can be quite a good place for this,
as it means you can be on hand to help them with
homework problems straight after school when the
evening meal is being prepared. If the kitchen does not
have enough space to house a small workstation, think
about other areas in the home, such as a landing,
hallway and under the stairs. These could all be turned
into good sites for compact workspaces, and they can
be used by other members of the family, too. A narrow
alcove or awkward corner in a small space will often
suffice as a neat workstation that can be hidden away
behind a sliding or hinged cupboard door. Technology
is moving so fast that the more space you can devote
to computers, games consoles and music equipment,
the better. In the same way that having more than one
bathroom was once deemed a luxury, so the multi-
computer household is fast becoming the norm.

RIGHT In a contemporary apartment, low-level living includes a
wall-to-wall desk that encourages work and play in equal measure.
A collection of beanbags and stools means that several children at
once can take on a number of different activities.

children of this age regard lava lamps as essential, but make sure that they're turned off by the time you go to bed at night.

Beds need to be adaptable for this age group. A single bed with a pull-out divan will provide additional sleepover space when friends stay over. A built-in cabin bed can also be created with a pull-out second bed. Bunk beds can be installed for children over six years of age, although you should encourage them to sleep in the bottom bunk at first. Provided that you have somewhere to store it, a fold-up camp bed is also fun for impromptu overnight guests.

Children of this age adore the unexpected, so a small play platform with a wooden railing provides a mini-stage, an enclosed space for creating dens or simply a private space away from a sibling. Changes of level within a room are a child's idea of heaven and one-off pieces of furniture such as a rocking chair or an inflatable chair add kudos and novelty, particularly when friends come to play. A large wall-mounted or freestanding mirror is a good idea, as a child will want to admire her dressing-up clothes or a new outfit for a friend's party. A simple dressing table can double up as a small desk in a restricted space.

Since children in this age group are straddling the gap between childhood and the teenage years, they may start to indulge in considerable amounts of floor-level living, lounging about on beanbags or on the floor itself, so make sure that it's comfortable. You could install soft and less durable floorcoverings but remember that, although your child is less likely to spill things now, the occasional set of muddy boots or bottles of nail polish will inevitably enter the scene and make their mark. In preparation for the teenage years, you might want to suggest sophisticated shutters or blinds to replace any window treatments that will soon be deemed too childish.

ABOVE Re-used furniture and contemporary wall shelves meld into a comfortable, cluttered child's space that is full of creativity and action.

OPPOSITE Two single mattresses are transformed into an ocean-going ship with the addition of a tree-trunk mast, a rope ladder and a suspended canvas sail. The other half of the room is a dedicated playspace.

A workstation can be a matter of a home-office-type desk housing a computer and drawers for paper, or a battered old school desk with storage within. Alternatively, a simple worktop may be installed along one wall and fitted out underneath with freestanding baskets, boxes on castors or filing cabinets.

Whichever type of desk you decide to go for, there will need to be a task light on the worktop. An uplighter may also be useful, for casting some indirect light. Clip-on reading lights that slip onto the top edge of a book are good for children in this age group, who usually read in order to drop off to sleep. Mini-flashlights are popular, too, for novelty value and for secretly communicating with siblings, sleepover chums or even neighbourhood children. Fashion-conscious

BATHROOMS

Increasingly, children have the luxury of their own bathroom off their bedroom, but in most families they still lay claim to the adults' bathroom.

SHARING A BATHROOM

Accommodating the clutter of children's bathtime in the adults' bathroom is a process that changes over the years. A baby really needs only a small, portable baby bath placed in the adult bath and, if there's the space, an area alongside for putting on her nappy once she's dry. This can be as simple as a changing mat placed on the floor, but a small chest of drawers or raised area within the bathroom is easier on your back. If your bathroom is tiny, it may be more practical to do this in the nursery or bedroom.

In the early days you need only a small area in the bathroom cupboard to store most of a baby's bathtime paraphernalia, such as towels and a couple of simple bath toys, as well as nappies, creams, spare vests and sleep suits. Keep bath toys in a simple bag that fixes to the wall or in a drawstring bag that hangs on the back of the door. Alternatively, buy an all-in-one unit on castors that will house toys, clothes and toiletries. A bath stool with a lid not only provides storage but is useful for older children as they can sit and dry themselves if you need to attend to their younger siblings. At the end of the session, everything can be stored in the stool.

As your child becomes more mobile and independent, you will need a safety mat in the bath, more interesting things to play with, such as mechanical water toys, and a flannel or sponge.

RIGHT A deep, modern bathtub is perfect for containing young children's splashes and toys. The painted and varnished floor is also resistant to a junior bathtime battering.

CHILDREN'S BATHROOMS

If you're planning a bathroom specifically for children, bear in mind that low-level fixtures and fittings look cute but they won't last forever. Their limited lifespan will mean an expensive refit once your small six-year-old becomes a strapping ten-year-old.

It's a good idea to keep accessories such as towel hooks and clothes rails within easy reach, while providing steps – either integral or freestanding – for easy access to the bath and wash basin. Indulge your sense of fun with the flooring: glittery textured vinyls appeal to both girls and boys, while underwater scenes and other images make exciting thematic backgrounds for the rest of the decoration.

A purpose-built child's bathroom is not the only alternative to a family bathroom. You may be able to squeeze a wash basin and vanity mirror into the corner

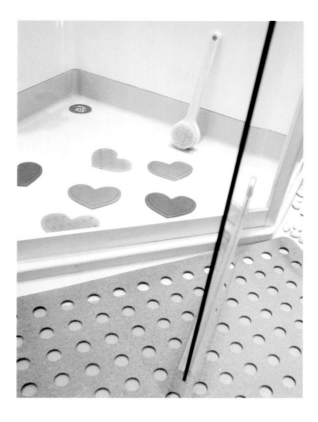

LEFT Heart-shaped non-slip mats are a decorative addition to a child's shower.

BELOW LEFT In a tiled contemporary setting a shallow sunken bath doubles as a waterplay area at bathtime.

of your child's bedroom, which will help considerably in easing the pressure on the family bathroom. A shower can often be incorporated in a downstairs cloakroom to create a child's bathing area as a family expands.

BATHROOM SAFETY

Safety is of prime importance when it comes to children and bathrooms. Make sure that the flooring is not slippery, and that the bath and shower have non-slip mats (these are useful for babies and toddlers alike). For toddlers, small steps that enable them to reach the basin taps safely are a good idea. The steps can also be used for climbing in and out of the bath.

A lockable, wall-mounted cabinet that is generous in size and placed out of children's reach is very useful. It can also double up as storage for harmful cleaning products, such as bleaches as well as medicines and sharp implements. Make sure that toothbrush holders and soap dishes are made from unbreakable materials.

MAJOR CHANGES

Once you have children, your home can start to feel very cramped. Not only does the storage seem inadequate but also there's no longer a quiet space for you to escape to should the need arise. Before you rush to move house, think about how you may be able to capitalize on your existing space. Your thoughts will probably turn to expanding your home in any direction possible, to create additional bedrooms or bathrooms, or extra living and working space.

CREATING EXTRA SPACE

First of all, think about how your family may expand, and anticipate what extra space you are likely to need. The two areas of the home that become most important when children enter your life are likely to be the kitchen and the living space. Where once cooking an evening meal for two was part of your leisure time, suddenly food preparation, consumption and clearing away can become a large part of your day, creating extra demands on your time. Children, especially younger ones, love to be where you are, so an area of the kitchen devoted to eating and simply hanging out becomes the main requirement of any home with restrictions on space.

Do you need to create a home office or a permanent guest room for other family members who visit regularly? Could you convert part of your child's bedroom into a homework space or turn a study into more of a family room once she starts school? Are there 'dead' zones that you can make more use of? Garages, understair cupboards and landings are often neglected areas that are good for converting into functional spaces. Although extending your home by building on or up into the roof is the most expensive way of creating space, it can transform your home and probably give you more space than you imagined

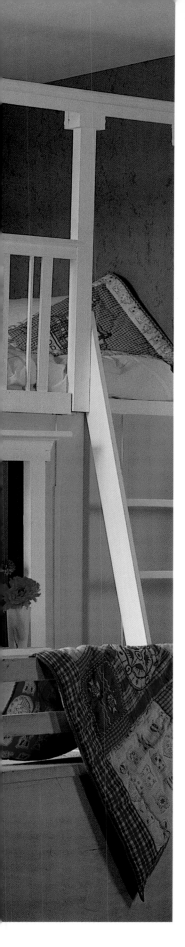

possible. Reaching out to the garden is also a good way of providing flexible living space. This needn't be in the form of a permanent structure; decking, awnings and arbours are all more cost-effective alternatives.

Make a list of which rooms in the home you use the most and for what. If the dining room, for example, is seldom used, consider turning it into a playroom or study. If you have a small kitchen next to a living room, think about knocking through to form a cooking/living space for the whole family. Two small bedrooms may be better turned into one larger shared one, fitted out with bunk beds and a small bathroom. If you have a garden, why not clear away the garden shed and replace it with a playroom? Alternatively, you could move your office to the garden from the spare room and turn that into a playroom.

If you are thinking of reconfiguring the space within a room or within the house itself, draw up a scale plan to get a rough idea of how your ideas will look in practice before obtaining quotations from builders, architects and suppliers.

USING PROFESSIONALS

Once you have analyzed your living space and decided on any major changes, it's time to call in the professionals for detailed guidance and advice on matters relating to building, plumbing, wiring and design. While you may be capable of putting up some shelves in your child's bedroom and assembling a flatpack wardrobe, when it comes to installing extra sockets for new technology, changing the lighting set-up, incorporating a wash basin or building a mezzanine bed or platform, it's safer and more efficient to get professional help.

Reputable builders are often booked up months ahead, so obtain quotations well in advance. Obtaining personal recommendations and then looking at work

already completed is the best way of finding the right builder, although there are professional organizations that list approved contractors.

A good architect will probably approach your space from an entirely different perspective from you and come up with ingenious solutions as well as accurate plans. These can then be submitted on your behalf for planning approval and supplied to builders for quotations. Make sure that you give the architect a tight brief to prevent any misunderstandings.

If you are reconfiguring your living area by knocking through rooms, an experienced interior designer will be able to come up with exciting ideas for organizing the space, storage suggestions and information about the choices you have for materials that fit your budget. A consultancy fee may be charged, but this will be offset against any uninformed decisions that you may make.

Discussing your ideas with professionals often gives you a clearer idea of the order of work, too, which is vital but not always obvious if you've never had any building work done before. There are builders who specialize in attic conversions, and architects and interior designers who have specific expertise and experience of family homes, so check these out first.

Budgeting for extending, building or reconfiguring is something you should think about from the start. You may have to compromise on some elements once you have costed materials, labour and furniture. Always add on a contingency figure of 20 per cent of the total cost; once a room has been stripped back to its basic structure, defects such as dry rot and poor wiring have a habit of revealing themselves.

LEFT Using all the available space from floor to ceiling is a good way of creating additional sleeping space in a small home. This ingenious design solution incorporates a platform bed with safety railings on top of a play house.

RIGHT Planning your
sleeping, storage and working
space before you embark on
any building work, or
commission tailor-made
furniture, will ensure that you
think of everything before you
commit to any expenditure.

MAKING A ROOM PLAN

When planning a child's room, bear in mind that even
the most unpromising of spaces can be improved,
provided that you take the time to plan. Above all,
be practical: there's little point in dreaming about a
mezzanine-level bed arrangement when you live in
a low-ceilinged apartment, or in planning a luxurious
chilling-out area in a room that is long and narrow and
needs to be shared.

Start by drawing a scale plan of the room on graph
paper to map out exactly the area you have to play
with. You will need graph paper, a pencil, a steel tape
measure, a ruler or scale rule and a calculator. A good
working scale is usually 1:25.

It will quickly become clear as you work if there are
any awkward or inflexible spaces in the room such as
the area between two doors or an odd-angled wall.
With a scale plan, you will find it easier to calculate
whether your existing furniture will fit neatly into the
space. Measure large pieces of furniture and make
cut-outs so that you can move them around the floor
plan to decide on their best arrangement. Think about
flooring and lighting at this stage, too. Effective lighting
can often disguise ugly or tiny rooms, while good
flooring can distract attention away from low ceilings
or an awkwardly shaped space.

Remember that gender and personality differences
will, to some extent, dictate how a room is planned.
For example, girls tend to like dressing-up games more
than boys, so they may appreciate a full-length wall
mirror before boys are remotely interested in their
appearance. Equally, a studious older child will want a
lot more space devoted to books than a child whose
main passion is football.

The following tips and sample room plans should
help you make the most of the space you have.

NURSERY

Contrary to the opinion of many department stores and furniture manufacturers, nurseries work best as simple, functional spaces. The basic requirements – cot, storage and display – will fit into even the smallest of rooms to make a cosy nursery.

- Position the cot or Moses basket away from draughty windows and doorways and also heat sources such as radiators.
- To make the most of the wall space, stand the cot along one wall, rather than having it freestanding in the room. Once babies can pull themselves up to stand, they feel safer when at least one side of the cot rests against a wall.
- A comfortable armchair is useful for feeding, particularly at night.
- If you'd like your baby to share a room with a toddler sibling, you might want to make a nursery 'corner' within an older child's room.
- A small sofa bed for you to sleep in may prove invaluable for those nights when your baby is particularly needy, to ensure that your partner doesn't miss out on sleep as well.
- Plan for different types of storage: for nappies and changing equipment, bedlinen, toys, baby shower gifts and clothes.
- A nappy changing area is essential but it could be as simple as a changing mat on top of a chest of drawers or table.
- A dimmable overhead light will help make your lighting more versatile.

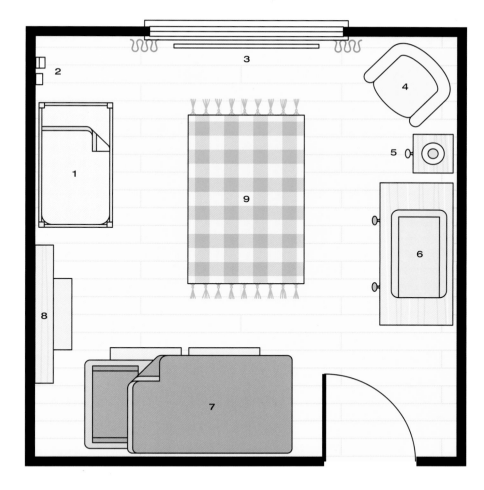

- A plug-in nightlight is invaluable for checking on your baby at night. A small table lamp positioned by the feeding chair is also very useful.
- If your toddler shares the nursery or if one parent occasionally sleeps in the nursery, a bedside table and light will prove invaluable.
- Have the socket for the baby alarm as close to the cot as possible.
- Practical flooring, such as painted floorboards, can be softened with a rug. Make sure that it has a non-slip underlay.

KEY

1 Cot

2 Baby alarm and plug-in night light

3 Window and radiator

4 Feeding chair

5 Table lamp with low-wattage bulb on small table

6 Chest of drawers with changing mat on top

7 Toddler's bed with storage underneath, or adult sofa bed

8 Display shelves with clothes cupboard underneath

9 Rug

SHARED SPACE

Rooms shared by children need to be flexible, since a baby and a toddler rapidly become a sports-mad child and a sophisticated but emotional pre-teen. The older they are, the more they will value having their own separate areas. After drawing up the floor plan, think about how you could create two distinct areas within the space.

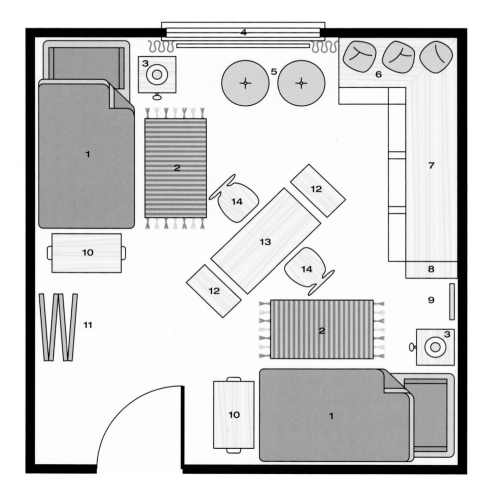

- Dividers such as screens, freestanding bookcases, desks on castors or curtains suspended from the ceiling are all good ways of creating separate zones.
- If there is enough room, consider dividing the sleeping space from the play area.
- If the room is small, choose bunk beds in order to save on space.
- A long, single desk area for homework with room for two chairs and storage underneath is a neat space-saving solution, as are hinged desks that open out from the wall and folding chairs.
- Built-in storage makes the most economic use of space, although this is obviously less flexible when two personalities decide their room needs reorganizing.
- Two of everything is one way of preventing arguments over territory and belongings in a shared room, but if you don't have the space, mobile furniture can prove particularly useful.
- Light sources should include a bedside lamp and a desk lamp for each child.
- Large rooms can probably take two matching single beds and bedside tables as well as freestanding storage such as a wardrobe or chest of drawers.
- A small radiator placed discreetly halfway up a wall can free up valuable floor space.
- When a nursery is shared with an older sibling, remember to include some toddler-specific storage, which can be beneath a freestanding or cabin bed or open shelving on the wall. Mobile toy boxes on castors are also a good solution, as they can be hidden away when not in use.
- Small shared spaces benefit from plain, unobtrusive floorcoverings to make the room feel larger.
- Two identical or similar rugs help to demarcate different zones within the room.

KEY

1 Bed

2 Bedside rug

3 Bedside table and lamp

4 Window and radiator

5 Seating area

6 Cushions stored on top of cupboard for extra seating

7 Built-in cupboards with integral steps that double as pull-out drawers

8 Open shelves at end of cupboards

9 Mirror

10 Storage trunk

11 Folded-up screen for impromptu room division, with pinboard on both sides

12 Mobile bookcase

13 Mobile desk

14 Desk chair

ATTIC ROOM

Rooms under the eaves of the house often make ideal children's rooms, with their interesting sloping ceilings and handy cubbyholes for games of hide-and-seek. Older children especially adore being at the top of the house, close to the sky and cocooned in their own cosy space.

- If possible, install a wash basin and toilet, perhaps even a small shower room or bathroom, to increase your child's sense of independence as well as freeing up your own bathroom.
- Use screens to separate the play area from the sleeping area.
- Make the most of natural dividers in the form of roof joists or eaves to create different zones within the room.
- If two children are sharing the space, place single beds under the eaves and leave the space in the middle, which is full height, for playing.
- Create the feeling of a mezzanine by building in cabin beds that incorporate steps up to them.
- Compensate for the lack of height by choosing low-level seating and divan beds.
- Position a desk under the eaves.
- Make the most of awkward but interesting nooks and crannies, such as on either side of the chimney breast. Create quirky storage solutions, like tailor-made shelves, pinboards and pictures fixed to sloping areas.

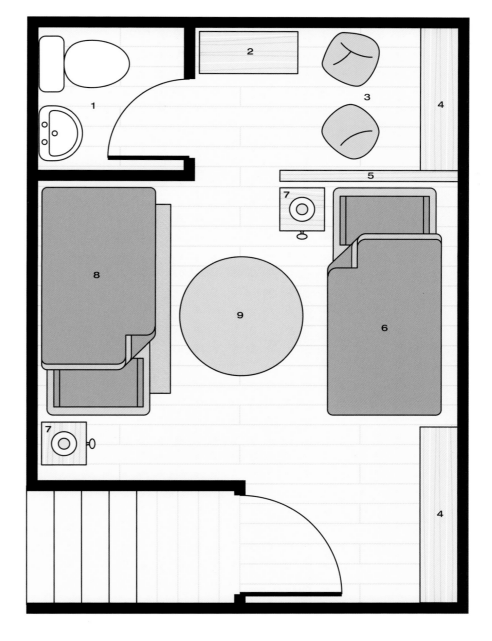

KEY

1 Separate room with wash basin and toilet

2 Freestanding toy storage

3 Low-level seating area

4 Under-eaves storage

5 Low screen to separate play area from sleeping area

6 Second bed, or fitted storage

7 Bedside table and lamp

8 Cabin bed with drawers/ steps

9 Rug

SQUARE ROOM

You are particularly lucky if you have a square-shaped room, as square rooms are often the most versatile of spaces to plan, lending themselves to being neatly divided, if necessary.

- Place a sink or shower in one corner and screen it off with an angled wall, if desired.
- Build in a row of wardrobe units along one wall, which will not alter the shape of the room too much.

- In shared rooms, place single beds along two of the walls, along the same wall or either side of the window for a dormitory effect.
- In a large square room you have the luxury of placing the furniture away from the walls and making a focal point in the middle of the room. In this way you will still have space to spare on the walls for freestanding or wall-mounted storage.
- Soften the angles in a square room by positioning rugs diagonally or using curved furniture.

KEY

1 Wash basin and mirror

2 Towel rail

3 Window and radiator

4 Miniature sofa for soft toys

5 Bedside table and lamp

6 Bed

7 Freestanding wardrobe

8 Long wall mirror, or pinboard

9 Desk with open shelving above, or a second bed

10 Chair

11 Dressing table, or chest of drawers

12 Bathroom mat

13 Rug

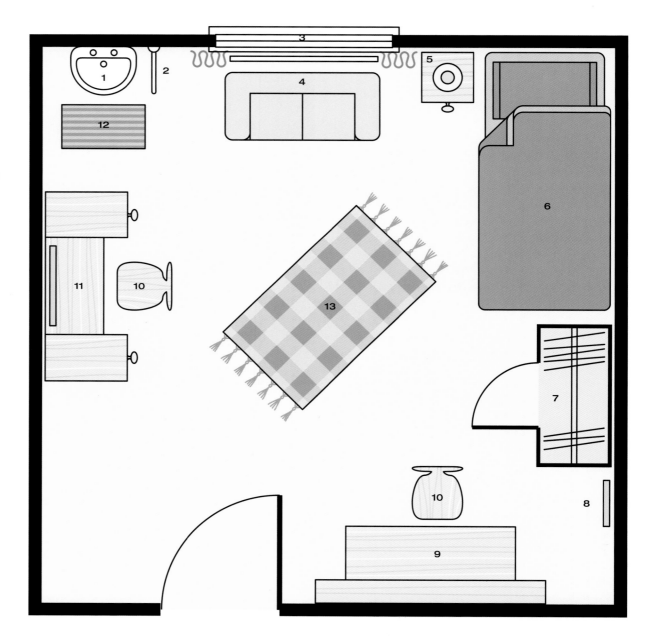

LONG, NARROW SPACE

This shape of room means that you have to be even more resourceful with your space. Use as much of the floor-to-ceiling area as possible, with full-height fitted shelving, for example, to capitalize on every inch of space, and employ a few visual tricks to make the room seem wider, too. One consolation of having such a limited room space is that children often become tidier as a result.

● Position the bed against one long wall and built-in cupboards for clothes, along with open shelving, on the other wall. This will free up playing space in the centre of the room.

● For a shared room, place two single beds end to end along one wall and build in storage below and above the beds. Alternatively, position bunk beds along one side of the room, with storage for clothes, toys and books on the other.

● Floorboards running across the room instead of down, or a rug with horizontal stripes, will make the room appear wider.

● Place a mirror at the far end of the room to bounce light back into the space.

● Paint the far wall a different and striking colour from the rest of the room. This has the visual effect of bringing the far wall towards you and pushing back the side walls, offsetting the 'tunnel' effect. A warm colour will enhance the illusion.

● Place a focal point, such as beanbags and a low table, at the far end of the room, to detract from the narrowness of the space.

KEY

1 Floor-to-ceiling fitted bookshelves
2 Built-in desk with storage underneath and shelves above
3 Desk chair
4 Clip-on shelf for books and lamp
5 Bunk beds with underbed storage for toys
6 Window and radiator
7 Beanbag
8 Low table or unit on castors
9 Built-in clothes cupboard
10 Noticeboard and shoe rack
11 Floorboards running across the room

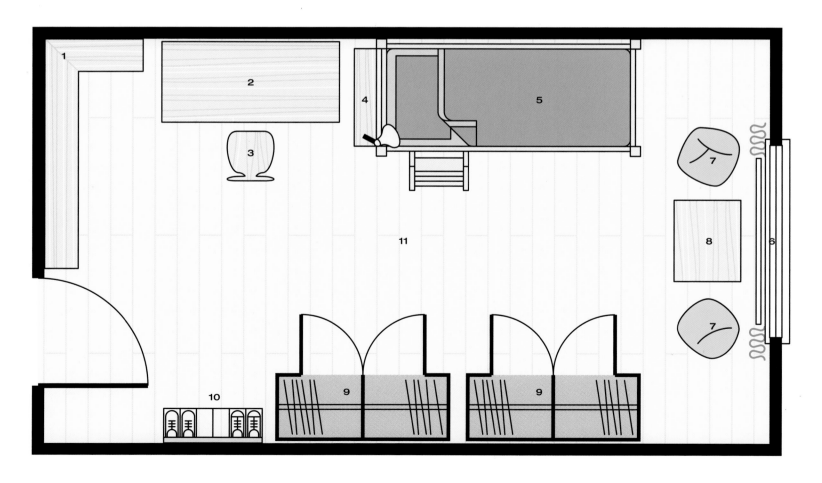

OPEN-PLAN LOFT LIVING

LEFT Ella and Leo each have one end of the room to call their own. Ella has her own workdesk with a display area above and peg rails to the side for storing large, bulky items.

RIGHT The attic room has been well planned so that both children have their own belongings close to hand.

Converted spaces, particularly attics, make interesting children's bedrooms. This shared bedroom is bright, spacious and practical, combining sleeping, playing and working space for Ella, aged six, and Leo, aged four. If you're adding a new room to your house or reconfiguring a space, plan the layout in advance to make sure that all the children's furniture, toys and technology can be housed neatly in one place. Here, bold panels of colour close to the beds distract attention away from the variety of sloping walls and ceiling.

After the shelves were planned, the bed positions were chosen, followed by the placing of the radiator benches. Planning the layout in this way meant that there was a communal playing space left in the middle of the room.

Rather than painting all the walls white, which can be tempting to do in an attic room where there are no obvious dividing lines for decorating, Ella and Leo were asked to choose a paint colour for their own bed area. Leo decided on orange, Ella on pink. The panels of colour add definition, interest and a sense of personal space for each child. Toys are tidied away under the beds in neat baskets and boxes, which allow for easy access.

The beds and furniture are painted blue – Leo is a keen junior decorator who lent a hand painting the wardrobe and the miniature table and chair, under close supervision, naturally – but the dividing shelves

As most of the bedroom walls turned out to be sloping, parents Heather and Winfried made the most of the available space by incorporating a room divider of open pigeonholes that follows the contours of the walls and acts as a display area, too.

The room divider was devised at the planning stage and was specially made to follow the roof line and act as a visual barrier between the two children's sleeping areas. In time, as the children get older, the plan is to divide the space completely in two by inserting frosted glass sliding doors, which will give the children privacy but still allow the light to filter through.

For the present, large toys and books fill the open shelves, which are accessible from either side of the room. Ella and Leo enjoy placing objects on the floor here but, once they've been tidied away, they usually leave them alone – apart from the books, of course.

ABOVE Under-bed storage baskets are great for hiding clutter and keeping small toys off the floor. Small tin trunks, sturdy fabric-covered cardboard boxes and mobile boxes fitted with lids and castors are also useful for containing an assortment of belongings.

LEFT Flexible furniture and fittings can dramatically increase the amount of play and living space in a room. This slatted wooden top not only disguises the radiator beneath but also provides additional seating for the children.

RIGHT Attic rooms often incorporate awkward angles and spaces, so it's important to plan the storage at an early stage. These open pigeonhole shelves are perfectly placed as a neat room divider that also offers storage opportunities.

The furnishings have been kept deliberately simple, so that they don't become outdated. Adaptable storage, such as large baskets and metal trunks, means that different things can be stored as time passes. Leo needs space for his toy garage and building blocks, while Ella has her dolls' house displayed on a painted chest of drawers that was once the nursery changing table. Under her bed there are baskets crammed with dolls and dolls' clothes; under his, construction bricks and toy cars.

Small-scale tables and chairs are invaluable during a child's early years. Ella and Leo generally sit at their table when they want to look at books, but they could also use it for messy play such as modelling clay and dough, drawing and painting. As the children get older, the table will still be useful as a flat surface for jigsaws and board games. Similar miniature tables and chairs are widely available from furniture stores.

LEFT A smart blue blackout roller blind, which helps the children go to sleep in summer, contrasts well with the orange-painted wall panel running around Leo's bed. The window space also provides a resting place for his soft toy collection.

OPPOSITE Painting furniture is a good way of introducing colour to an attic room, where neutral walls help to disguise sloping ceilings. Wicker baskets provide practical and attractive storage for toys under Leo's bed, which is also home to a rolled-up futon mattress for sleepovers.

are painted white so that they merge into the adjacent wall. A small wooden chair, painted pink, doubles as a bedside table for Ella, while a low radiator with a chunky beech top doubles as a seat for the children and their soft toys.

A sisal carpet in neutral grey is practical, hardwearing and easy on the eye, but undeniably a little scratchy on bare feet. For that reason, rugs have been placed by each bed to soften the surface and placate the children.

Winfried and Heather kept a close eye on the future when they planned their children's room. A boy and a girl sharing a room is perhaps the greatest challenge of all because the room needs to cater not only to different ages but also to widely differing interests, which become more and more pronounced as the children get older.

LEFT Leo enjoys using the desk and chair for playing with his toys and for reading. His mother painted the furniture and made the chair cushions.

sorted & stored

THINKING AHEAD

The mantra for children's storage is 'plenty of it, wherever you can put it'. Whether you choose industrial-looking stacking crates, country-style baskets or painted wooden chests, tidy-up time will be that much easier once all the paraphernalia of childhood is sorted and stored. As soon as your children are old enough to understand that all their belongings have a place of their own, you are on your way to establishing tidy habits in them.

Children seem to collect toys and amass clothes in a manner that is out of proportion to their physical size. From day one, when you buy nursery equipment and special furniture for your small baby and receive gifts from family and friends, you begin to realize what an impact this new generation will have on your living space. Extra storage is always needed at this stage, and each new milestone in your child's life brings with it fresh demands.

When children are small, storage and display often converge in a celebration of small-scale, colourful objects. Of course, there is an alternative version of events, too – a horrible mishmash of gaudy plastic toys, infuriatingly small construction components and a mound of soft toys with no home to go to.

Enjoy the initial stage of this small but perfectly formed set of belongings while your child is at the nursery stage, when everything is easy to contain and often more in tune with adult tastes. Choose storage that captures the appeal of first shoes, tiny dresses, smart sailors' hats and fluffy towels. You could start with two or three small wall-mounted pigeonholes, then add to them when your child is at the toddler stage, until you have a whole wall of storage.

Instead of spending hours applying a *trompe-l'oeil* decoration to the main wall, fix up a couple of painted shelves and display treasured baby objects, painted

ABOVE Improvised freestanding storage has been created from painted wooden fruit crates stacked one on the other. For safety purposes, these crates are best screwed to the wall so that they cannot be pulled over.

LEFT A degree of flexibility in the design of this built-in, invisibly supported chunky shelving allows the height of the hanging rail to be adjusted or the shelves to be converted to drawers as the child gets older.

RIGHT Fabric-lined baskets are useful for nappies (diapers) and towels, as well as toys and toiletries, and are easy to transport from room to room.

LEFT Miniature furniture is never out of use for long. Once your children are too big to fit into their small chairs, their soft toys soon colonize the space.

LEFT Detachable wall storage is a versatile way to contain small objects, from hairclips and headbands to miniature soft toys, playing cards and lost pieces of board games. Use canvas bags, calico drawstring bags or small baskets attached to the wall with chrome coat hooks.

RIGHT Simple lines and plain colours produce a tidy, controlled playspace, proving that plastic crates can look stylish after all. A low-level bench houses a variety of foam shapes that can be used as playthings or seating, while the space beneath is large enough to hold fairly deep crates.

RIGHT Wooden peg rails are useful for all ages. Fix them to the wall at lower levels for smaller children and gradually add more, higher up the wall, as your child grows. Keep the lower ones in position for shoe bags and sports balls and use the higher ones for rucksacks, bags, hats or cycling helmets.

boats, favourite teddies and books as a form of storage that doubles as decoration. Create hanging space for clothes by fixing a rail underneath a shelf or by suspending wooden poles from the ceiling (see pages 84–5). Peg rails are useful for hanging and displaying colourful outfits and hats or for drawstring bags filled with cotton wool (absorbent cotton) and nappies (diapers). Fabric pockets can be hung from the wall for a similar purpose or for keeping soft toys free from dust. They can be used later on for smaller toys such as playing cards, flashlights and cars.

Generous baskets lined with fabric make good places for keeping frequently used items such as nappies, towels and changes of clothes. And don't forget the toys. Pigeonhole shelves save on hunting around in a cupboard or drawer, while wooden boxes on castors have a toy-like quality about them. Transparent plastic crates keep things tidy but also visible, and are easy to lift.

Once your baby becomes a toddler and his friends are invited around to play, his bedroom will become a toy-dumping ground if you're not careful. A few hooks or a peg rail placed low on a wall can be a handy way of storing frequently used objects such as a toy doctor's kit, miniature fold-up buggies and drawstring bags filled with pretend food or building bricks. You can also use them for hanging clothes such as dressing gowns. By putting the storage at toddler height, there is a greater chance that your child will feel inclined to help tidy up.

Having a playroom is a luxury that means you are able to store many large toys, board games and small items of furniture away from the bedroom. Floor-to-ceiling cupboards are the neatest option, together with low-level access so that your children can quickly reach what they're searching for. A combination of shelves, cupboards and drawers is the best option.

A whole wall devoted to built-in shelving and incorporating an easy-clean worksurface for messy play is ideal. A small sink will make clearing up less of a chore after a painting session.

Utility storage often comes into its own in children's spaces. Old lockers, painted wooden crates that have been sanded smooth, tin boxes and plywood drawers all look good combined with colourful walls and painted floorboards. School-age children enjoy helping with the decorating, so try allocating them an object of their own to paint. Have some MDF (medium-density fibreboard) cubes made up for painting. They come in handy as bedside tables (invaluable storage for books and a flashlight), as extra seating when friends come to play, and as small tables on which to play cards and board games.

As children approach the pre-teen years, their storage needs develop accordingly. The homework corner increases in importance and using the family computer becomes a more frequent activity. If you prefer to monitor your child's computer use, you could keep the technology elsewhere, such as in a playroom or den, or in a general family space such as the kitchen or dining area.

As schools use computers more and more, it's likely that as your children get older they will need to have their own equipment in their bedroom. You can prepare for this time by having a wall of custom-built shelving for books and a purpose-made desk. Although an immovable solution, it does allow you to store all the relevant technology and make space for stationery and accessories.

Bigger children mean bigger everything, from clothes to equipment for sports and hobbies. Look up to see if there is any unused space above your head for cupboards to store items that are not needed often or for bookshelves above doors.

Safety is always a consideration when you're planning storage for children's spaces. Make sure that freestanding furniture such as bookcases or small cupboards cannot be pulled over by adventurous toddlers or pre-school children. It's safest to fix these items to the wall. Watch out for trailing flexes (cords) if you place lamps on bedside tables or in shelving units or computer on desks. Check renovated furniture for jagged edges and avoid using glass for shelves.

OPPOSITE A wall-mounted pole housing a large roll of paper prevents the regular question of 'got any paper, mum/dad?' Labelling children's storage boxes with a picture of their contents or a child's photograph is something the children can create for themselves.

ABOVE Self-contained pigeonholes provide generous storage and display space on a blank wall. A desk can be as simple as a length of wooden or laminate worksurface fixed under a windowsill.

TYPES OF STORAGE

There are basically two different types of storage: built-in and freestanding. Built-in storage works especially well in small rooms because you can design it exactly as you wish and use every inch of available space. If you are planning on moving in the near future in order to increase your living space, then freestanding storage that you can take with you may be the better option. Freestanding storage is generally cheaper than built-in storage.

BUILT-IN SOLUTIONS

The best materials for built-in storage are wood and MDF (medium-density fibreboard), although specialist materials such as steel and iron have their place in contemporary settings. Walls of storage and shelves blend into the space best if they're painted the same colour as the walls.

Make the most of any structural features, particularly if you are short of space. Alcoves are ideal for multi-purpose storage. A hanging rail fitted into a small alcove is a good idea for small-scale clothing, but make sure that there's enough space underneath for when your child's bigger. The higher parts of an alcove may be fitted with pigeonhole shelves for bulky items and bedding, the middle area with two chunky shelves and the lower portion fitted with a temporary clothes-hanging rail and low shelves or open space for shoe racks and toy storage. For older children it's worth considering turning an alcove space into a homework area by building in a small worktop and fitting shelves or cupboards above and below.

If you're building in hanging rails and shelves in a nursery, keep an eye on the future. Provide some low-level shelves so that toddlers can reach their toys. You can always fit a fabric covering, roller blind (shade) or cupboard front to these at a later stage. Built-in cupboards for clothes, toys and spare linen are always neat storage options, which can be made more versatile by fitting them out with flexible innards for maximum adaptability as your child grows. For a seamless and timeless appeal, keep the cupboards plain and simple. You can choose from a variety of door fronts, including flush fitting, panelled, glazed or panelled with wooden fretwork, chicken wire or metal gauze or grilles, depending on the style of the room. Have fun and add interest with handles and pulls. Try animal shapes, small integral rope handles, miniature footballs and seashore motifs. It's much easier and cheaper to swap handles and repaint cupboards than to rip out very stylized storage units.

Beds with built-in storage are especially useful in small rooms. Apart from the obvious under-bed drawers, you can buy or build bedheads with integral shelves, cupboards and lighting.

Under a window, you could fix a low-level worktop that doubles as a nappy-changing area and slip deep baskets underneath for storage. The same worktop will in time become a desk then a window seat, which will make useful storage for seldom-used items such as spare blankets and duvets, forgotten sports equipment and Rollerblades. In a playroom or family space, fit a low-level table/desk with a lift-up lid for storage and play. When space is limited, consider a fold-down desk that incorporates some wall storage

Built-in shelves range from 'invisibly' fitted chunky display shelves to simple, Shaker-style ones and rustic sets of three or four shelves. In a contemporary setting, fit small drawers within a chunky shelf for additional accessories storage. Pigeonhole shelves give you the choice of fitting baskets or plastic crates into the space or using the gaps for housing single items or a small book collection. Start off with larger pigeonholes at the bottom and decrease their size as

you go further up the space for smaller objects. When you're designing a whole wall of shelving keep an eye on scale. Store bulky, deep items at the bottom on wider shelves and reduce the depth of higher shelves. Fit rails or pins so that the shelf heights are flexible and can be swapped around as needed. Remember, too, that shallow drawers are easier to keep tidy and arrange than deep drawers, which tend to gather extraneous and unwanted belongings.

Fitted shelves above doors are particularly useful for displaying precious objects or striking accessories, while open box shelving fitted to walls is neat and versatile. In small spaces, a narrow shelf running all around the room at picture-rail height is useful for breakable objects. If there is space, fit deeper shelving to create storage for soft toys and hats. If you have wall space either side of a door, then you could fit shelves right across the room, including above the door. Open storage looks best if your child is tidy by nature; otherwise, you can always hide a lot of toys behind closed doors!

Most girls from the age of six will appreciate some kind of dressing table, so a mirror cut to fit a space and mounted flush on the wall can form the basis of a custom-built grooming area. Fix two narrow shelves to the wall and install slim drawers in between for jewellery and nail polish. A narrow peg rail either side of the mirror will provide hanging space for feather boas, hats and dressing-up clothes. A small wall-mounted cupboard next to the mirror provides another way of storing jewellery. Alternatively, fix an old printer's type box, readily available from junk shops, to the wall for miniature treasures.

LEFT Chunky shelves look graphic and help turn this corner into a proper work area. Placing them above the table and chairs also 'fixes' the shelves so that they don't appear to float.

LEFT Cabin beds offer endless possibilities for storage under the bed base. This one is painted white, with a nautical flourish added in the form of underbed curtains to form a seaside cabin, complete with cut-out window. Younger children will create spontaneous houses, shops and toy bedrooms under a bed like this. Alternatively, fill the area with stacking boxes, baskets, bookcases or small chests of drawers for additional storage in a small space.

RIGHT Plastic contemporary storage boxes double as stools in a smart playroom. Their depth makes them particularly useful for storing large items.

CENTRE When only designer accessories will do, a small office filing cabinet makes the perfect accompaniment to the *Jack Light*, designed by Tom Dixon, in the foreground.

FREESTANDING SOLUTIONS

Simple bookcases and flexible shelving systems are the easiest to adapt to a child's room, regardless of their age. You can paint untreated timber to match the walls and blend in to the space or choose a material that fits in with the overall look.

In nurseries, small cupboards with solid or glazed doors look charming and they are often large enough to contain changing equipment and clothing. Extend the life of a half-size wardrobe or armoire by converting a low-level hanging rail into shelving for an older child's collection of T-shirts, jumpers, skirts and trousers. Cabinas (fabric-covered wardrobes) are good temporary or permanent solutions in small spaces, as they are both decorative and functional.

Once you've sorted out the clothes, there are the toys to consider. As soon as your child is mobile, toys are picked up, played with and discarded in most rooms of the house, so portable storage is essential.

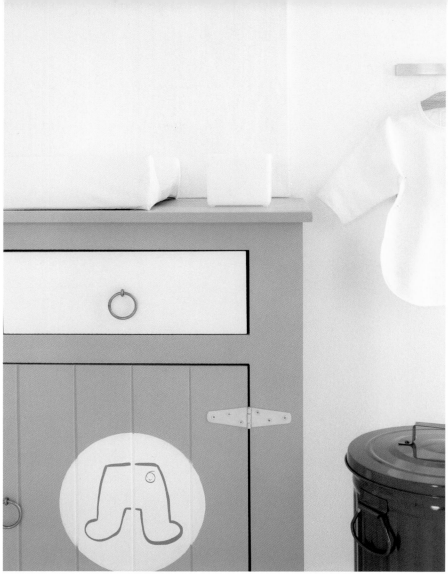

Baskets, plastic crates, or wooden or sturdy cardboard boxes labelled and stacked on shelves or in a wooden 'filing' system are indispensable. Keep the items that are played with most frequently at a low, easily accessible level. Toddlers and older children enjoy making their own labels, either with drawings or letters. Laminate their efforts and make them into luggage labels that tie onto the containers, or else stick them to the front of plastic crates. For very orderly children, try colour-coding containers: blue for bricks, red for roads and transport, and so on.

If there is not enough space in a child's room for everything, then a portable wire-basket storage system can be used under the stairs, in downstairs cupboards

ABOVE Customize and update junk furniture by painting it with clear, muted colours and add striking motifs such as baby joggers or a baby face.

and even behind living room curtains for a discreet and portable playroom. It is easy to tidy away at night, too. A log basket filled with toys and fitted with an inner drawstring bag is a good way of disguising gaudy plastic and would be as suitable in the living room or kitchen as it would in the bedroom or playroom.

Storage on castors is easy to transport, but bear in mind the safety factors: a child will see a wooden crate on wheels with a lid as the ideal place for dumping a younger sibling and transporting him out of your sight. However, mobile storage is undeniably practical, so make sure that the castors are lockable and your child understands that the box is for storage only.

Under-bed boxes or drawers on wheels are good places for toys and games, small dolls and construction kits, and they also double up as animal hospitals and car garages. A sturdy toy box in a bedroom is always made more versatile with the addition of castors and rope handles. Choose from junk finds such as old luggage trunks, tea chests that you can customize or a purpose-made toy chest with handles. This also becomes a useful prop for imaginary games, assuming the role of a pirate ship, a woodland den or a hospital bed at the drop of a dressing-up hat.

Clothes rails on castors are available in child sizes as well as adult versions. They make good movable storage for dressing-up clothes (see page 77) as well as purely functional wardrobes in scrupulously pared-down contemporary spaces. A stack of plastic drawers of varying sizes is also ideal for sorting belongings, and these, too, are available on castors.

Older children often love industrial metal shelving, which looks good in conjunction with metal filing cabinets. Adult-size desks are good for older children who accumulate paperwork, school books, photographs and keepsakes, while plan chests are useful for storing drawings and artwork.

ABOVE Custom-made storage is often less expensive than bought pieces and can be built to suit your child's room. Here planked toy trunks are a crisp alternative to the traditional pine toy chest.

OPPOSITE Simple shop-bought shelving may be personalized in a variety of ways. Paint it to match the bed or walls, covering the shelves with plastic or fabric, or paint it in contrasting colours and drape it in muslin or bright canvas – it will quickly become a child-centric but useful piece.

STORING SMALLER ITEMS

Drawstring bags can be indispensable for storing all sorts of smaller, lightweight items in children's spaces, from the nursery to a pre-teen's room. As well as being practical dispensers, they can form part of the room's decoration. For example, in the nursery, hang the bags from hooks or rubber suckers, school cloakroom-style, in neat rows of three or four, to hold cotton wool, nappies and toiletries.

Vary the sizes of the bags to fit your children's belongings. Use peg rails to display a series of matching or neatly contrasting bags. By positioning the rails at an accessible level your children will be able retrieve their own possessions, and they may also be encouraged to tidy up after themselves.

Toddlers love to open drawstring bags and find building bricks, dolls' clothes, small cars and trucks or miniature railways inside. You can also use drawstring bags for small items of clothing, such as underwear and socks, and for favourite books, and for storing at-the-ready sleepover kits for older children.

ABOVE Dressing-up clothes are best stored where they are easy to access and replace. A shelf placed above a hanging rail provides display space, too.

ABOVE RIGHT A bedside table that includes multiple drawers will hide all sorts of clutter, inevitably leading to a tidier bedroom.

Little toys and dolls can give you storage nightmares if you have no small spaces to pack them into after play, so small-scale sorters are vital. Ideal for this kind of storage are fabric pockets strung onto wooden dowels or small metal chains and hung on the backs of doors, from a top bunk, even underneath wall shelves. Alternatively, eyelets can be inserted at the corners and they can be hung from hooks fixed to the wall or ceiling. Fabric pockets are also useful on the back of doors for shoes and slippers. Personalize the pockets with your child's name, or what's stored inside; felt letters in bright colours machine-sewn onto calico pockets look crisp and cheerful, while bright fabric pockets can be finished off with patterned motifs denoting the contents. Collections such as key rings, cars or dolls can be signified by attaching one of the collection to each pocket, either by sewing or with Velcro or iron-on fabric adhesive.

As your child gets older, you will notice a gradual gathering of tiny but treasured objects. These include initials on neck chains, hair accessories, playing cards and collectors' cards, small metal vehicles and important horse-chestnut swaps. Miniature chests of drawers are invaluable for storing such fiddly things that can drive a parent to distraction. They are also perfect for keeping safe mysterious but important-looking pieces from board games and jigsaw puzzles, rescued from the vacuum cleaner at the last minute. A noticeboard is also useful, keeping photographs, party invitations, artworks and mementoes out of the way but easily accessible.

RIGHT Larger families really benefit from individual storage for each child, and drawstring bags are an incredibly versatile way of storing a variety of things. Hats, scarves and sports shoes are among the regularly needed items that might otherwise end up on the floor. Identification labels are essential if you have a collection of bags.

LARGE TOYS AND EQUIPMENT

You can't beat a huge toy cupboard fitted with deep, generous shelves for board games and large stand-alone toys such as cash registers, push-along animals and fold-up playtents. The bigger the space you can devote to one cupboard, the better.

Craft materials need to be kept together and out of reach of small children. Keep them in a lockable glazed cupboard or a small child's suitcase, which is appealing both visually and practically, perched on a high shelf. Paintbrushes and paint tubes stored upright are easy to find placed in baskets within pigeonholes.

Freestanding easels that incorporate a lockable space for paints, together with a roll of drawing paper, are comprehensive storage units that can be transported from the bedroom to the kitchen or playroom and back again.

Movable clothes rails, just like those used backstage in the theatre, are good solutions for dressing-up clothes, ballet tutus and all the other paraphernalia that goes with imaginative play. Suspend fabric shoe hangers and pouches from the rail for storing accessories such as scarves, jewellery, wigs and false moustaches, feather boas and glass slippers.

OPPOSITE Older children really appreciate having a place of their own in which to work. Mobile storage enables them to move their school work out of the way when friends come around to play.

LEFT Rolls of drawing paper can be quite bulky, so consider hanging them on ropes attached to the wall or ceiling, ready for toddlers' doodles and spontaneous art moments.

ABOVE Old shop fittings make great cubbyholes for artists' materials in homes where toddlers on the loose could cause havoc to older siblings' belongings.

RIGHT An unremarkable wardrobe is dramatically jazzed up with Memphis-style geometric patterns in this retro-style bedroom. Pockets of varying sizes, hanging above the desk, swallow up all manner of odds and ends.

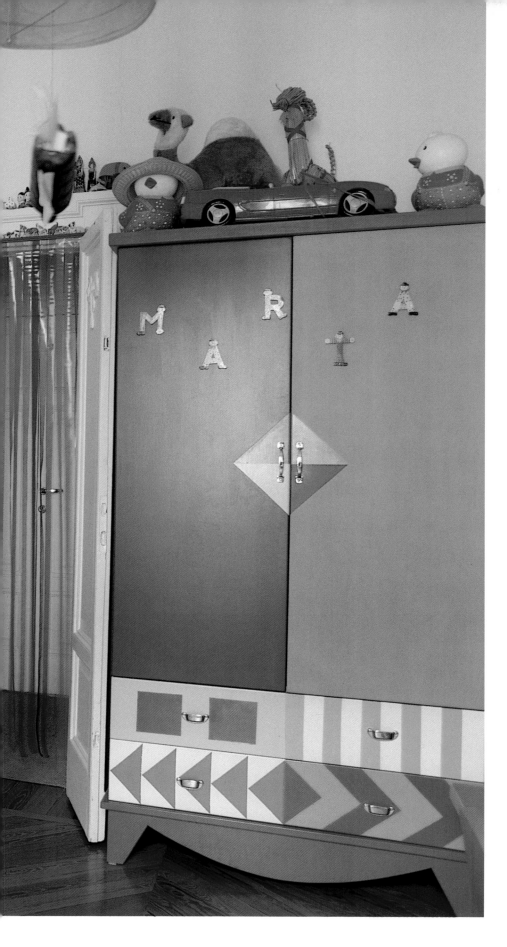

Paint old hat boxes or cardboard boxes for storing hats on the footrail and you have an instant, transportable dressing-up unit.

Footballs, tennis rackets and Rollerblades need to be accessible and easy to find. Keep rackets in an umbrella stand in the corner of the room, or make a feature of them by putting them in fishing nets suspended across the ceiling. (For a less obtrusive look, insert eyelets into calico sheeting, and lash it to hooks in the ceiling.) Alternatively, hang rope netting across one corner of the ceiling for bats and balls. A plastic-lined drawstring bag is a good way of storing wet and muddy football boots, while Rollerblades are best kept in a lidded box. Skateboards can be suspended from metal hooks sunk into the wall so they resemble shelves. Hats look good hung in a row above them. If you want to keep the equipment out of sight, try making a tall, narrow space within a wardrobe for stacking rackets and boots.

TECHNOLOGY

Each year seems to bring with it new technology for children's rooms. If you're fighting the temptation to install a television in your child's room, you may have already given in to the idea of a games console and/or computer instead. At the very least you will need to accommodate a ghetto blaster or mini hi-fi. Bring in the technology by dedicating a corner or alcove to a desk plus shelving that will accommodate everything. And remember the accessories – stationery, compact discs, DVDs, cassette tapes and electronic games. Plan out the space and allow for future new additions.

Computers can be kept on a small desk. If space is tight, fit the screen onto a swivel that swings out from an alcove. If two or more children share a computer, consider a trolley on castors that can be wheeled from one space to another, as and when required.

STORAGE WITH STYLE

Storage is an important element of a child's room if you want to create a place where your offspring can play, work and tidy up independently of you. Ten-year-old Hannah's bedroom is a simple, orderly space where a few key pieces of tailor-made and bought storage contain and catalogue all the everyday clutter. The room is a welcoming and cheerful place where her friends feel instantly at home and relish visiting.

LEFT A storage drawer with castors beneath the bed keeps Hannah's collection of shoes hidden well away and the floor free from clutter. Providing sufficient storage in your child's bedroom means that there's a greater chance of the room being kept tidy.

LEFT Hannah would have loved to have painted the entire room purple, but a compromise with her parents resulted in palest lilac for the walls to give a neutral backdrop. She was allowed to choose the colours used elsewhere, and opted for shots of lilac, purple, pink, mauve and violet for her favourite storage drawers. The drawers are designed to keep safe her treasured collections of small objects. The worktop above is curved around one corner of the room and is used as a desk, complete with laptop computer. Underneath the desk, a neat and generous space is given over to storage boxes on castors.

Hannah was very involved in choosing the colours in her room and coming up with ideas for how to store her collections of small but precious items. A set of square drawers is painted chequerboard fashion in a medley of colours and housed beneath a custom-built desk. The drawers hold all sorts of small bits and pieces – hair accessories, mini puzzles, games and tricks, jewellery, make-up and needlework among them. Hannah's strong creative streak is evident all around the room, from the interesting colours under the desk to the carefully decorated mirrors that hang above the bed. The drawers also neatly hide a radiator that sits beneath the window.

Castors have been used on most of the storage elements, to provide mobility and flexibility. The slim drawer under the bed holds Hannah's shoe collection, while the mobile crates under the desk roll out to

ABOVE Practical and pretty wall shelves and peg rails were fitted right around the room when Hannah was small. Now that the room has been extended and Hannah is no longer a toddler, they have been retained along the two walls above the worktop as a useful storage and display space.

ABOVE A bookcase on castors to accommodate Hannah's mountain of books is positioned close to the bedroom door, but it can be moved easily whenever a change of layout is required, such as for sleepovers or to aid cleaning.

RIGHT Hannah's father built the carcass for this mobile cupboard and slotted in ready-made drawers for storing folded clothes. A roller blind is fixed to the top of the cupboard and can be pulled down to protect the clothes from dust.

LEFT Ready-made storage drawers have been neatly combined in an MDF frame to create an appealing storage chest. Painted in colours chosen by Hannah, the drawers also give the desk a colourful focal point.

night. Her father made both units from MDF, which he painted purple (Hannah's favourite colour). The desk fits snugly around one corner and is curved to provide a neat work space. Painted pale lilac, it is unmistakably a girl's work area.

The bedside table is actually a drum given to Hannah by her father after a trip to Carnival in Rio de Janeiro. Occasionally it provides an extra instrument in musical interludes that take place alongside serious dressing up with friends.

The storage ideas used in Hannah's bedroom are all hugely successful and innovative, but also inexpensive. Hannah's parents chose simple materials, such as MDF, and transformed them with colourful paint, castors and tailor-made frameworks. The bedroom that they created with the help of their daughter is a functional but highly personalized space that Hannah, as well as her friends, loves being in.

reveal brimming dressing-up boxes containing glitzy fabrics, glamorous feather boas and tiaras for when friends come to play.

Hannah likes the fact that everything in the room has a place of its own, so it's always easy to find what she wants. Elements of the room have stayed the same since she was a toddler. The bed was her first one, an Eastern European pine sleigh bed, painted white, and the peg rails and shelf once ran right around the room when it was a nursery and before the room was extended. The rails are still useful for storing hats and bags and for displaying small ornaments, toys and pieces of Hannah's artwork.

Sleepovers are important to older children, and Hannah's bookcase and wardrobe are fitted with castors so that they can be moved out of the way to accommodate a fold-up bed when friends stay for the

RIGHT Deep boxes fitted with castors, are perfect for storing dressing-up clothes and toys. The boxes have no lids, making it quick and easy to access the contents and to tidy up afterwards.

NURSERY CLOTHES RAIL

Simple, neat and economical on space, this charming hanging rail is ideal for a nursery, keeping clothes on display yet out of the way.

In small spaces such as a nursery where there may be room for only one small chest of drawers, a neat hanging storage system doubles as display and practical storage. Clothes are easy to see and simple to access and, when not in use, they provide visual interest for babies. Ribbons of different colours are used to suspend the wooden dowelling, which can be painted to match the colour of the room. Alternatively, use lengths of ribbon all the same colour and add bows, rosettes or flowers in contrasting tones for a different look. Tie a bow around the bottom of each coat hanger hook for a pretty extra touch. If the ceilings are high, you could increase the amount of storage by using two or more lengths of dowelling.

MATERIALS AND TOOLS

✽ Wooden dowelling, approximately 1m (3ft long)
✽ Tape measure ✽ Small wood saw ✽ Wood primer ✽ White water-based emulsion (latex) paint and brush ✽ Length of softwood, approximately 1m (3ft) long and 8cm (3in) wide ✽ Pencil
✽ Bradawl (awl) ✽ 10 brass or chrome screw hooks
✽ 12mm (½in) wide satin ribbon in different colours
✽ Drill ✽ Screwdriver and screws ✽ Rawlplugs
✽ Child-size coat hangers, painted white

1 Cut a piece of dowelling to length using a small wood saw. Apply one coat of wood primer and leave to dry. Next, paint on one coat of water-based emulsion (latex) and leave to dry. (You could use eggshell paint instead if you prefer a glossier look; opt for an organic or low VOC-rated version, if possible.) Repeat the process for the softwood hanging panel. Mark the position of the screw hooks on the hanging panel with a pencil and use a bradawl (awl) to make a small hole on each mark. Here, the hooks were positioned about 10cm (4in) apart. Screw in the hooks by hand.

2 Cut strips of ribbon to the same length – approximately 60cm (2ft) – and tie them into neat and secure bows around the dowelling rail. Make the bows the same size, and space them evenly along the rail.

3 Using a drill and screwdriver, attach the hanging panel to the ceiling or wall with rawlplugs and screws at either end. Next, take the dowelling rail and stretch out the ribbon ends along a flat surface to check that they are all the same length. Cut to fit if necessary. Tie the other end of each ribbon into a bow on the screw hook. Once the entire rail is in place, check that it is hanging level. If necessary, adjust the bows at the screw hooks for a perfect finish.

ABOVE This type of hanging storage could easily be adapted to create a completely different look in an older child's room. Swap the pastel-coloured ribbons for wire, thin white rope or metal chainwork. Brightly coloured clothes are decorative in their own right and add zing to a neutral space.

DRAWSTRING BAG

A sleeping bag will roll up small enough to fit neatly inside this practical denim bag, making it perfect for an older child to take on a sleepover.

This bag is large enough to hold a sleeping bag, and pyjamas, a washbag and a change of clothes can be slipped into the generous pockets around the side, which fasten with Velcro. The base of the bag is made from a waterproof fabric, which is very useful if the bag is taken on camping trips and put down on wet ground. You can make up the bag to any size you want; this one measures roughly 45cm (18in) high and 86cm (34in) in circumference. It's a good idea to wash the denim before you start sewing to stop the colour running as you work with it.

MATERIALS AND TOOLS

❊ ½m (18in) glittery plastic-coated fabric ❊ Fine pen ❊ Bowl or plate, measuring 27cm (10½in) in diameter ❊ Tape measure ❊ Scissors ❊ 1m (1yd) denim fabric 90cm (36in) wide ❊ Pins, needle and white basting thread ❊ Sewing machine and blue and white thread ❊ Eyelet (grommet) kit ❊ 2m (2¼yd) drawstring cord ❊ Sticky tape ❊ Safety pin ❊ ½m (18in) calico (heavy muslin) ❊ Iron-on Velcro ❊ Iron ❊ Images for transferring ❊ Scalpel (mat knife) and cutting mat ❊ Iron-on wet-release transfer paper

base – following the fine pen line as closely as possible. Remove the basting stitches. Machine-sew the side seam, and remove the basting.

For the top hem, turn over 1cm (½in) of the fabric (wrong sides together) and machine-sew. Measure 6.5cm (2½in) from the top edge of the bag down the side seam, and 1cm (½in) out from the seam on either side. Mark these two points and, following the kit instructions, attach an eyelet (grommet) at each point. Attach two more eyelets at the bottom of the bag, each one 1cm (½in) away from either side of the seam.

To make the casing for the drawstring, turn over 5cm (2in) of the fabric (wrong sides together) and machine-sew, leaving a 5–7.5cm (2–3in) gap at the seam for the cord to be threaded through. Cover both ends of the cord with sticky tape to stop them from fraying. Push one end of the cord through one eyelet and attach a safety pin to it. Thread the pin and cord through the casing until the cord appears at the entrance again. Remove the pin and push the cord through the second eyelet so that both ends are visible. Machine-sew the gap in the casing closed. Next, thread the cord through the two eyelets at the bottom of the bag, remove the sticky tape and knot each end. Turn the bag right side out.

1 To make the base of the bag, place the plastic-coated fabric right-side down and draw around the plate with a pen. Measure and mark an extra 1cm (½in) all around the circumference for a seam allowance. Cut around the outer circle.

2 From the denim, cut out a rectangle 90cm (36in) wide by the intended depth of the bag plus an extra 1cm (½in) for attaching the denim to the base and 6cm (2½in) for the top hem. Here, the rectangle measured 90 x 55cm (36 x 21½in).

Attach one long edge of the denim to the base (right sides together) with the pins at roughly 1cm (½in) intervals. Baste together along the inner pen line with white thread. Pin the denim ends together, forming a tube, with the seam allowance measuring about 2.5cm (1in). Baste.

3 Clip small Vs all around the base every few centimetres with scissors. Machine-sew around the base of the bag using blue thread – the small Vs will help ease the fabric around the circular

4 For the pockets, cut out calico rectangles to the desired size, allowing 1cm (½in) seam allowances all around. Turn under the seam allowances and machine-sew the pockets onto the bag using white thread. Iron the Velcro onto the inside of the pockets and to the bag in the corresponding positions. Cut out each image and, with the wet-release transfer paper, iron the image onto the pockets, following the manufacturer's instructions.

ARTWORK TUBES

These wall-hung storage tubes are ideal for keeping your children's artistic endeavours in pristine condition, protected from sticky fingers and spills.

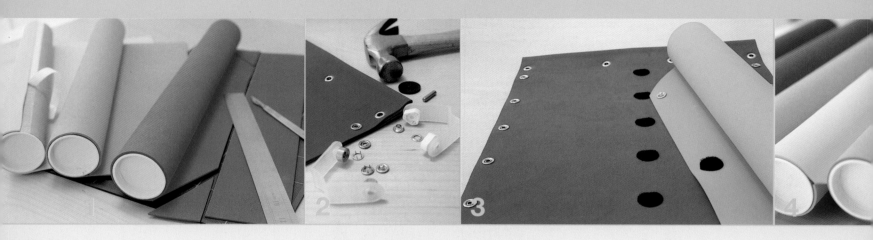

Simple and inexpensive to make and easy to use, these colourful tubes are the storage answer to those loose pictures and paintings that usually end up creased at the bottom of drawers or behind cupboards. They look equally good hanging on a bedroom door or on the wall above a desk.

If the room has a particular colour scheme, keep the storage simple by using only one or two colours. Cardboard tubes with lids are available from post offices or stationery suppliers, while the multicoloured neoprene sheets used to cover the tubes are sold at artists' suppliers. If you wish, attach an additional panel of neoprene with eyelets (grommets) to the backing sheet at the bottom of the tube run and fix on crocodile clips for storing and displaying wet paintings.

1 Take a sheet of neoprene and measure out enough to cover a tube, and allow a hanging edge of 5cm (2in). Cut off the top two corners using a scalpel (mat knife) and steel ruler. Attach the neoprene to the tube using two strips of double-sided tape. Repeat for the other four tubes.

2 For the backing, take the second sheet of blue neoprene and with a pencil mark out the position of the four eyelets (grommets) for hanging the cord, using the first tube as a positioning guide. (If you plan to store a lot of artwork in the tubes, you may want to use two sheets of neoprene to give the backing extra strength.) Mark the positions of the poppers (snaps) an equal distance apart, which is about every 6cm (2½in), down both sides of the sheet. Fix the flat halves of the poppers to this backing sheet for holding the

tubes in position. Fold the top edge of the neoprene under to form a 4cm (1½in) border. Following the manufacturer's instructions, fix the eyelets across the top of the backing sheet, knocking them into place with a hammer. (If you have never used poppers or eyelets before, practise beforehand on some spare neoprene.)

3 Fix the other halves of the poppers to each end of the covered tubes, so that they will line up with the matching halves on the backing. On the back of each hanging edge in the centre of each tube and in the corresponding position on the backing sheet, fix a Velcro circle for extra support.

4 Attach the tubes to the backing sheet using the poppers and Velcro. Thread the drawstring through the eyelets and knot the ends at the back.

MATERIALS AND TOOLS

❋ 1 sheet each of
45 x 30cm (18 x 12in)
neoprene foam in
green, yellow, orange
and red, and 2 sheets
in blue

❋ 5 postage tubes
with lids, each 44cm
(17½in) long

❋ Scalpel (mat knife)

❋ Pencil and steel ruler

❋ Cutting mat

❋ Double-sided tape

❋ 10 haberdashery
poppers (snaps)

❋ 4 eyelets (grommets)

❋ Hammer

❋ 5 Velcro circles

❋ 1m (1yd) strong red
drawstring

MOBILE STORAGE UNIT

This ultra-modern storage unit fitted with lockable castors not only solves the major problem of where to keep all your child's toys but also doubles as a seat.

A canvas cover slots over a foam pad and is secured with eyelets and turn fasteners to form this comfortable padded seat with two built-in storage boxes. You can make the covering extra-durable by using plastic-coated tablecloth fabric instead of canvas, or by treating the canvas to make it stain-resistant before making it up. If space is tight, make a single box in the same way. If you'd rather not make the box part of the unit yourself, use existing sturdy wooden boxes, sanding them back if necessary.

MATERIALS AND TOOLS

❈ 1 sheet of 2.5 x 1.2m (8 x 4ft) MDF (medium-density fibreboard) 15mm (⅝in) thick ❈ Steel ruler ❈ Wood glue ❈ Screws and screwdriver ❈ Bradawl (awl) ❈ 8 heavy-duty lockable furniture castors ❈ Wood primer ❈ White emulsion (latex) paint and brush ❈ Rectangular piece of 7.5cm (3in) thick, flame-retardant foam cut to fit unit top ❈ Canvas fabric, measuring approximately 1 x 1.5m (3 x 5ft) ❈ Scissors and pins ❈ Sewing machine and white thread ❈ 12 chandler's turn buttons, consisting of button mechanism, 2 oval eyelets (grommets), screws and nuts per turn button ❈ Soft pencil ❈ Scalpel mat knife and cutting mat ❈ Pliers

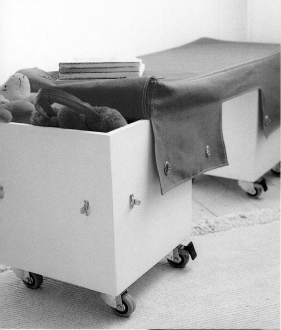

Make up two boxes by gluing and screwing together five squares of MDF (medium-density fibreboard), so that all the sides of the boxes measure 32 x 32cm (12½ x 12½in), to form two open cubes. With the help of a bradawl (awl), screw in a heavy-duty lockable castor to each corner of the two boxes.

Cut out a plank of MDF, measuring 90 x 32cm (36 x 12½in), to form the lid of the unit. Cut out two more pieces of MDF, measuring 28 x 14cm (11 x 5½in). Glue and screw one of these to the underside of the plank, so that the long edge of the piece is 2cm (¾in) from the edge of the plank and the shorter edges of the piece are the same distance from the sides of the plank (see the illustration on page 180 for guidance). Repeat with the second piece at the other end of the plant. These will allow each box to slide out to the side to half its width once the castors are unlocked, so that you can retrieve items from inside the box without disturbing the cushion seat. Apply wood primer, then paint the boxes and lid white. Cut a piece of foam to the same size as the plank and lay it in position on top of the lid.

To form the cover for the cushion, cut out five pieces of canvas according to the shapes illustrated on page 180, so that they correspond to the dimensions of the lid, plus a seam allowance of 1cm (½in) all around. Pin the fabric flaps to the top piece (right sides together) and machine-sew. Turn under the seam allowances on the raw edges, and stitch. Place the cover snugly over the foam.

Put the fabric cover and lid in place on the boxes. Mark the position of the turn buttons on the boxes as well as on the fabric. Fix six turn button mechanisms to each box with screws and nuts, starting off the holes with a bradawl. To attach the eyelets (grommets), offer them up, one by one, to the canvas and mark their final position with a soft pencil by outlining the inner oval shape. Remove the fabric cover and cut this shape out carefully with a scalpel (mat knife). Place the eyelets that have prongs attached through the oval cut-outs. Offer up the flat ovals to the other side of the canvas, so that the prongs can be bent outwards with pliers to fix the eyelets in position.

decorating

CREATIVE TIME

Whether you are creating a nursery from scratch or revitalizing an existing room, decorating a child's space is one of the most entertaining and creative aspects of being a parent. You can really be inventive in a child's room and know that your offspring will appreciate your efforts. What's more, now that children are becoming increasingly interested and involved in designing and decorating their own rooms, the process is assuming more importance as a shared activity. In many families where both parents go out to work, decorating is one area where everyone can get involved and indulge in creative time together rather than pure daily routine.

How to decorate your child's space is the first decision that needs to be made, so consider these key factors: the age of your child and how long you want the decoration to last; whether the space will be shared with another sibling now or in the future; whether the space will occasionally double as a temporary guest room for adults; and your personal style – whether colourful or muted, patterned or plain, glamorous or utility.

Once you've thought about these basics you can set about selecting a style, a theme and materials. However, this is probably not as straightforward as you might imagine because in recent years decorating children's rooms has come into its own, and all sorts of materials designed specifically for children are available. You really are spoiled for choice when it comes to deciding on wallpapers, borders, bedlinen and lighting, even paint. Whereas once upon a time you had only to choose a wall colour, now you can buy metallic, magnetic, glitter and scented paints, too. Walls no longer just hold up the house and separate rooms – they can also be blank canvases or large blackboards, even natural pinboards for those with

ABOVE Mesh panels inserted into junk furniture are decorative additions, but can also be quite revealing of their contents. Luckily the lilac walls and floor and pink cart also grab the attention.

RIGHT Wooden shelves painted to blend in with the walls are offset by pure white elsewhere in the room. Informative posters, such as maps, football charts and wildife identifiers, can often become an intrinsic part of a colour scheme.

collector genes. Other surfaces, too, offer plenty of scope for decoration. Storage and doors, furniture and floors, fabric and accessories can all be painted, appliquéd, découpaged and stencilled in a limitless stream of different styles, colours and finishes. This chapter guides you through the looks, the choices and the practicalities for encouraging your own creativity and that of your children.

ABOVE Furniture and walls painted in a riot of colour provide a relatively easy way of cheering up tired decoration and old pieces of furniture. Children's rooms can often bear clashing or loud colours better than their grown-up counterparts.

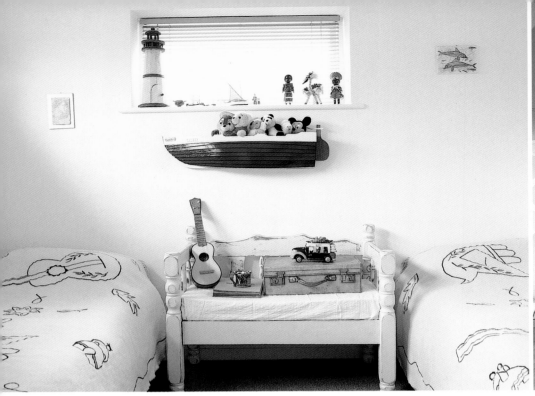

ABOVE Junk shop finds often give a more sophisticated feel to a child's room than purpose-made children's furniture. Here an old child's sofa is used as a bedside table.

ABOVE RIGHT This 1960s retro nursery has been created with a minimum amount of furniture and a very generous use of geometric-patterned wallpaper, instantly solving the dilemma of what to hang on the walls.

STYLE AND COLOUR

There is always a temptation to go wild in a child's room, emblazoning it with murals, busy patterns, themes and bright colours. However, restraint can be a good thing, particularly in a nursery where you want to create a comfortable and inviting environment for babies, and if you'd like to avoid redecorating every year or so. If you start off with a simply nursery, it's easy to build up layers of colour, furnishings or storage as the years go by. If the decorating impulse does overcome you, though, think about devoting maybe just one wall to a mural or motifs – it's easier and cheaper to cover over one wall when your child grows out of the theme or you tire of the décor.

Rather than slavishly following one designer's fabric or furniture collection, strive for the eclectic. It can be much more original and appealing to celebrate authenticity and seek out one-off pieces such as vintage toys or furniture to create a personal style. Once these basics are in place, it is possible to add some designer wallpaper on one wall or a signature cushion for an interesting melded effect.

When decorating a nursery, the choice of colour is, of course, entirely up to you as a parent. Keep it simple by using pale tones, and introduce colour with accessories. You may find that your baby's clothes, toys and a few objects such as pictures, window coverings and painted furniture are all that's needed to inject interest and colour into the room. Once your child is older, a neutral backdrop will allow her own artworks and belongings to influence the room's style.

All children adore definite colour and often yearn to see their whole room drenched in saturated oranges, greens, blues or yellows. If you cannot bear to paint all the walls in such dominating shades, you can still achieve a strong sense of colour by having bright accessories such as duvet covers, window blinds (shades), painted furniture, lampshades and rugs in one tone and keeping the walls more neutral. Two children sharing a room may have different preferences, so you can accommodate this by painting two of the walls, say the ones nearest to each bed, in a different but toning colour. This will also help demarcate a personal space for each child.

Two-colour schemes work particularly well in children's spaces. Apple-green walls look fresh and lively with red or cream bedlinen and detailing. Rose-pink walls and pale pea-green woodwork are a sophisticated feminine combination, while metallic beds with strong turquoise or lilac walls are a pre-teen's dream. Encourage your child to choose at least one of the decorating colours so that a sense of teamwork emerges. This will also give you the opportunity to negotiate your way out of any unreasonable decorating requests she may put forward in the future.

ABOVE Older boys like
nothing more than a splash of
red, white and blue for a
colourful but sophisticated look.
Apply the colour to bedlinen,
rugs and accessories so that
the bed can remain solid and
traditional. The stars-and-
stripes motif introduces a
strong graphic note.

PICKING A THEME

Choosing a theme for a child's bedroom can make
planning your decorating easier and provide plenty of
novel ideas for accessories and details. Most of the
enduring room themes involve elements that apply
equally to wall decoration, furniture colour, fabrics and
novelty beds or storage. Traditional boys' favourites
include knights and castles, witches and wizards,
football, cowboys and pirates. Girls tend to go for
fairies, ballet, cowgirls, the circus and animals.

If you have a boy and a girl sharing a room, you will
need to be circumspect. General themes that appeal
to both include marine life, the jungle and outer space
(see pages 114–17). Older children often prefer more
nebulous concepts such as geometrics, groovy
splodges, industrial or American diner chrome, or
favourite television characters. If the idea of such a
definite look fills you with dread, then think of other
styles you might want to encourage: vintage floral
fabrics will be pretty and understated in a girl's room,
while a dormitory look, which has become very
popular with boys since Harry Potter evolved into
such a literary icon, may appeal. Alternatively, you
could tap into your child's own hobbies: enthusiastic
collectors may be inspired by a seashore theme or
transport motifs, for example.

DECORATING WITH PAINT

The most economic and effective way of decorating for children is with paint. Washable surfaces are a bonus for the early years and will conserve the life of whatever scheme you choose. If you use traditional historic paints, you may want to add a coat of matt varnish to protect the surface, as the chalky quality of this type of paint shows up fingermarks very easily. If your family has a history of allergies, try using organic paints (see pages 134–7).

Paint technology is moving on all the time and there are now many specialist paints to try, including magnetic paint for noticeboards, murals and chair-rail-height borders. Metallic paints are available in many colours and add interesting texture to small, dark rooms. Apply them in square, chequerboard panels or borders for decorative interest or create a bull's-eye on one wall using different colours or textures. Paints that smell of citrus or raspberry are recent arrivals on the market but bear in mind that their novelty value will last a limited period of time.

Glitter paint is a fun innovation that brings space travel and pixie dust into the decorative mix. It can be applied over a new paint surface for a glittery finish and detailed with metallic pens.

Mixing one or more colours in a room is particularly popular in children's spaces. Using one colour for woodwork and another for the walls is a good way of brightening up an otherwise dark or small room. If you decide to use a very strong, deep colour on the walls, remember that it will take as many as three or four coats of a lighter colour to cover it up completely when you want to change the scheme.

Murals are another way of using paint in interesting ways. It is often best to restrict the picture to only one wall as you and your child can become overwhelmed with a scene that engulfs the whole room.

Fixing white-painted tongue-and-groove panelling – all around the room up to chair-rail-height and topped with a narrow shelf, or across the whole of one wall from floor to ceiling – will add a decorative flourish to a room. The shelving can then be painted either to match or to contrast with the panelling or the rest of the room. Dividing walls in these ways helps make the ceiling in a tall room appear lower, while the vertical lines of floor-to-ceiling panelling have the opposite effect, making the ceiling seem further away – a useful device in a room that isn't quite high enough and feels claustrophobic. Placing shelves higher up a wall also gives a sense of height.

LEFT It's hard to resist painting something pink in a girl's room. If you haven't the heart to create an entirely pink palace, then indulge the girly phase by really going for it on a piece of furniture. Use gold, silver and magnetic paint, plus glow-in-the-dark stars for true indulgence and enjoyment.

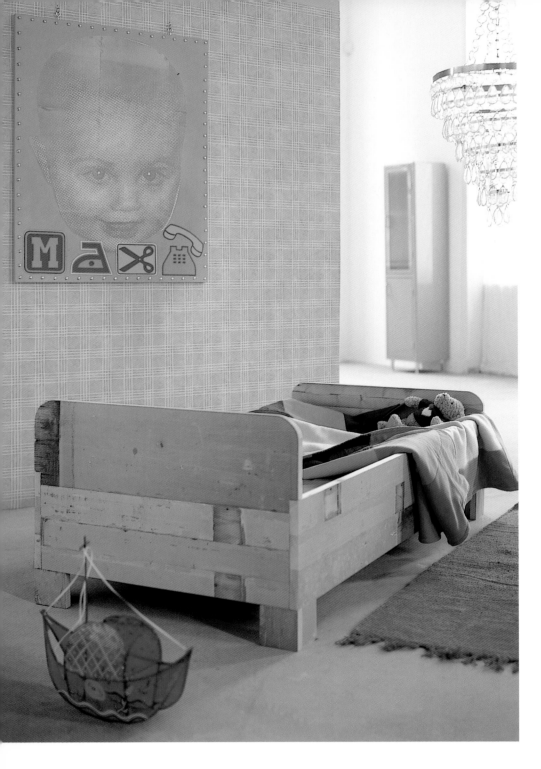

ABOVE Young children will love having giant enlargements of their baby photos on their bedrooms walls. Enhance the portraits with symbols that children will recognize and a border of upholstery pins or brass fasteners.

WALLPAPER AND BORDERS

Although it's been out of fashion for such a long time, wallpaper is enjoying a revival. There are new and interesting textures and finishes available, and even traditional wallpaper such as anaglypta is undergoing a change of image. Contemporary designs include mosaic tiles, textured wood, generous geometric shapes in varying textures and photographic scenes of landscapes, together with the usual collection of storybook characters and cartoon heroes, some more obviously tasteful than others.

Wallpaper often loses out over lined and painted walls, though, purely because it is easier to grow tired of. But it can be useful as a tough, wipeable surface. For a new approach to old techniques, try papering only one wall of the room for a bold statement.

Novelty or decorative borders are a way of adding character to a small child's room, but once you decide to change them, the process can involve having to redecorate the room completely. Use them with care and, if possible, choose those that peel off easily.

NOTICEBOARDS

All children from around the age of three enjoy having an area of wall devoted to their own endeavours. A large cork pinboard painted the same colour as the walls lasts a long time and makes a versatile display area for original artworks, party invitations and photos. Frame it with a painted cardboard border for younger children and swap it for a wooden frame later on. Older children may appreciate a fairy-light border and a discreet peg rail above the board for displaying sports medals and similar awards.

Corkboards can be combined with an area of thick-grade plywood or MDF (medium-density fibreboard) sprayed or painted with blackboard paint. Although the spray is more expensive than the paint, it is quicker and easier to apply. Provide a drawstring bag or a shaped gulley fixed to the wall below the board for storing blackboard-friendly pens. Magnetic paint can be applied under the blackboard paint for attaching important messages, fabric swatches and secret notes from friends. A battery clock fixed to the board or displayed nearby brings a sense of purpose and organization to the whole area.

If you prefer a noticeboard that can be hung on the wall, you could make one from MDF and cover it with a thin layer of wadding and felt or fabric, to go with the other furnishings in the room. Wipe-clean boards are a good idea for younger children.

ABOVE A thin picture rail placed halfway up the wall makes a convenient place for displaying children's artwork in a playroom. A colourful panel painted at the bottom adds further definition to the wall.

ABOVE LEFT Panels painted onto the wall with blackboard paint at child height make good drawing stations for the pre-school age group.

RIGHT A collection of soft
toys doubles as a colourful
display against a sky-blue wall
in a child's nursery. The
handmade cot quilt simply adds
to the multicoloured effect. On
the wall, a painted peg rail of
beach huts is almost hidden by
the children's clothes and
accessories hanging from it.

INVOLVING THE CHILDREN

Children thoroughly enjoy being part of the decorating
process, and there are ways of achieving this without
opening a huge can of paint, handing over a
paintbrush and running for cover. However, while it can
be fun to decorate a child's room as a family activity, a
professional will get the job done more quickly and
probably with less stress.

Even children as young as two can be involved in
decorating their own space. Together you can cut out
animal shapes – heads, body and limbs – and connect
them together using brass fasteners to create a string
of party animals to hang from the ceiling or across the
room. Fairies, footballers or ballerinas could all be
made in the same way. For decorating windows, cut
out snowflake and flower shapes using a mixture of
coloured tissue paper and plain white paper, and
border them with black paper. They will look like
stained glass when fixed to the window pane.

Other decorations, which can be festive or simply
colourful, include paper chains made from discarded
wallpaper, and paper shapes fixed temporarily to the
wall. Blown-up photographic images of the children

could be attached to the wall along with their names
and some 'thought bubbles'. Simple motifs, such as
trains, daisies, lorries, people or footballs, can be
painted directly onto the wall. Blank canvases,
available by mail order, are ideal for older children to
express themselves with paint, either to create pictures
or to paint plain panels of colour or geometric shapes
in their favourite shades.

Artwork created by the children themselves can be
displayed in a variety of ways. A run of jute rope or
metallic cord plus miniature pegs is ideal for displaying
artwork that quickly loses its unique appeal when the
next day's offering appears.

Encouraging your child from the age of about six
to look at paint charts will help her develop her own
sense of colour. Devote a scrapbook to decorating
ideas and encourage your child to cut out favourite
pictures from magazines. She will quickly become
fascinated by mixing colours, photographic images
and found objects, such as feathers, leaves and
pebbles. Pointing out how closely nature and colour
are intertwined will teach her to be more observant
about her surroundings.

Another good way of encouraging children to create
something of their own for a room is to make picture
frames for their favourite images and photos. It is not
beyond a child of five or six to paint up a simple
wooden picture frame and decorate it with sequins,
shells or miniature footballs.

Découpage can be used to decorate all sorts of
things, from small objects to larger pieces of furniture.
It is a cheap and easy process with instant results that
uses scraps of wrapping paper or other found images
from magazines. Mix up one part PVA glue to two
parts water, brush it onto the back of the paper and
stick the paper in place. Leave to dry, then apply a
coat of the PVA mix over the top as a sealing coat.

LEFT Sloping rustic ceilings need little decoration. This attic room holds an oar along one rafter and a clothesline for displaying finished artworks. Along the limited wall space sit open bookshelves and a fold-up work table. The seats of metal stools have been decorated with animal and flower designs.

RIGHT Painted
chequerboard flooring is
relatively easy to achieve. Mark
out the floor accurately before
you start painting, and be sure
to choose colours that will not
dominate the room.

CENTRE Sometimes the
floor itself provides most of the
decoration in a room. This
playroom floor in linoleum
provides a warm orange/red
glow underfoot.

FLOORING

Stripped and painted floorboards complement small
rooms, especially nurseries. White and other pale
tones produce a muted effect that can make a small
room feel larger, and, if you want to, you can
embolden the space with a bright rug. Use exterior
water-based wood paint or eggshell topped with a
layer of matt varnish for extra toughness. Painted
floors can be made to resemble tiled ones by applying
a chequerboard design in two or more colours. Stripes
in different colours on each floorboard also liven up a
room, as do circles, stepping stones and a simple
painted 'rug' in the middle of the room.

Practical and economical flooring solutions include
cork tiles, rubber flooring and natural linoleum, which
has anti-bacterial qualities. They are all warmer
underfoot than conventional vinyl floors and are simple

and quick to maintain. Make them easier for children to live with by adding a rug or runner. This will bring comfort as well as making a crisp decorative statement in a sparsely furnished room.

Painted canvas floorcloths are another way of providing a more comforting material for a plain floor. Use emulsion (latex) or acrylic paints to decorate the canvas with hopscotch numbers, snakes and ladders or a variety of animal motifs. Once you've applied the design, seal it with a coat or two of matt acrylic varnish to protect the surface. (Masking tape will help you to produce straight lines.)

ABOVE Pink glittery linoleum tiles with a slightly textured surface make a fun as well as practical floorcovering for a child's bathroom. A rug or runner will help soak up any splashes from bathtime, at the same time softening the surface.

FURNITURE

The bed is usually the centrepiece of a child's room, so it pays to make it look as appealing as possible, especially at bedtime! Headboards offer many possibilities for theming the decoration. Painting or staining the headboard or cutting out fretwork shapes and shaping the headboard and footboard into crenellations, domes or waves will create a distinct style. Simple wooden or MDF (medium-density fibreboard) headboards can be padded and covered with fleecy fabric or felt for a soft and welcoming backdrop. For the more ambitious, whole bedframes can be made from MDF and shaped into cars, boats and trains, then painted with authentic detailing. It will make bedtime a far more attractive proposition for reluctant sleepers.

Painting furniture is a good way of disguising battered pieces of storage and restoring unappealing or discoloured wood to a sleeker state. Setting up a first nursery often involves painting an old chest of drawers so that it blends in with the overall decoration. In children's spaces, you can personalize and add interest to individual pieces of furniture by fixing on painted handles, applying découpaged shapes (see page 102) or attaching wooden motifs with wood glue. Stencilling and specialist paint finishes are other good methods of converting dull pieces of furniture into something more interesting.

Basic dressing tables, freestanding screens and miniature chests of drawers are available as MDF blanks and can all be transformed with colourful paint. Eggshell and water-based emulsion paints are the best types of covering for this work, while *trompe l'oeil* decoration can add a fun, whimsical element. And you don't need advanced painting skills to paint a chest of drawers so it looks as if a football sock or skipping rope is hanging out of a drawer.

ABOVE Stencilled wall flowers have strayed as far as the daybed in this daisy-heaven playroom. The same stencil has been applied to the wooden frame of the daybed and then cut out with a jigsaw.

CENTRE The subtle, neutral decoration in this playroom has been carried onto the miniature, white-painted table and chairs.

FAR RIGHT A sea of colour and motifs extends from painted furniture to lampshades and a mosaic mirror in a nursery that is nothing if not visually stimulating.

Once you have repainted a surface you can leave it as it is or add motifs, images and textures by using stencils, découpage, coloured tape, sticky-backed plastic and iron-on fabric panels. Geometric shapes and spots always look jazzy. Get children to paint their own motifs onto small sets of drawers and help cover small peg rails with a couple of coats of paint; the peg rails can be nailed to the wall or slipped beneath a set of wall shelves.

Miniature furniture in the form of raffia-seated wooden chairs, small tables and work chairs and freestanding storage will all benefit from a paint treatment. Personalize chairs with the names of children and their dates of birth, and add motifs according to their personalities. Alternatively, create a cohesive look by painting two or three objects such as a dolls' wardrobe, a small rocking chair and a tiny chest of drawers in the same colour, then add flowers, trains or fairies, to suit the mood of the room.

BEDDING AND SOFT FURNISHINGS

Using fabric in the nursery and a child's room is a good way of introducing some decorative detail without going down the totally coordinated route. For a newborn baby you will really only need several cot (crib) sheets (flannel and fitted are the cosiest and easiest to use) and a cellular blanket for winter. You could add a muslin canopy above one end of the cot for rustic appeal. Patchwork quilts, fleece blankets and soft woollen cashmere throws are perfect for providing extra warmth and visual interest. They last and last, too, and they can also be used in a pram or buggy and on the floor elsewhere in the house for lying on, or for sitting on once your baby is bigger. In time, they become playmates and comforters for older children, and then graduate to being used for making soft toys and dolls.

ABOVE Floral fabrics and cotton gingham make a pleasing partnership in a girl's bedroom. Boys may prefer stripes and dots.

RIGHT Muslin canopies are simple to hang and provide instant decoration in a bedroom or playroom. Regularly spaced decorations around the rim and at the apex lend definition.

Homemade cot and bed duvet covers can reflect more accurately your choice of colour and style – and they are more economical to replace when your child outgrows them.

If you cannot resist nursery-style motifs, restrict yourself to making a floor cushion, or pelmet and tiebacks for the curtains rather than giving in to floor-to-ceiling indulgence. Toddlers, and older children, too, love floor cushions and beanbags, which come in for a lot of heavy use. On bunk beds there are further opportunities for adapting the bed dressing to suit the room. Calico or canvas sheeting tucked under the top mattress provides an enclosing canopy or den for the bottom bunk, which can be decorated with appliquéd patches of camouflage fabric, metallic fabric shapes for a bit of sparkle or animal-print fabric panels for a safari-chic approach.

Canopies above single beds include the ever-popular fabric panel. Liven it up with a band of fake flowers laced with fairy lights or multicoloured fabric streamers to give a sense of the circus, or sew random shapes onto the muslin itself.

Quilts and fleece bed blankets provide neat focal points for the room. Either engage in a riot of colour or keep them muted, according to what else is going on in the room. Blankets can be made more useful by sewing on pockets for storage (see pages 120–1), while patchwork quilts can be created from scraps of clothes that the children have outgrown, to make a lasting heirloom.

Cartoon, book, TV and movie characters are a real influence on a pre-school child, so one way of accommodating a child's taste into your carefully considered scheme is by giving in and buying a gaudy duvet cover. They're not usually expensive and if you can't bear the sight of them during the day, simply cover them with a subtle rug or throw, and remove it just before bedtime. The same 'cover-up' theory goes for favourite football teams and particularly un-adult colour combinations, such as pink and black, that children of this age seem to adore.

For the child who views bedtime as a challenge to stay awake, establish a regular nighttime routine and follow up a bath with a bedtime story between really cosy flannel or jersey sheets, duvet cover and pillowcase. These soft, inviting fabrics have just the same effect on children as they do on adults, making them more likely to snuggle down and drift off to sleep. In the winter, a warm hot water bottle enveloped in fleece, linen, fake fur or a knitted cover will add to the comforting feel (see pages 152–3).

Miniature furniture can be dressed up with fabric, too. Simple basketweave chairs and sofas look good enhanced with fabric-covered foam cushions trimmed with buttons, fabric ties or frills. A few drawstring bags made up in the same fabric and hung on peg rails will create a gentle cohesion rather than slavish coordination, which always seems to look out of place in a child's bedroom. Another subtle way of drawing together the room is to appliqué shapes or motifs onto a simple cotton rug or window blind to blend in with fabric used elsewhere in the room. Wall hangings or quilts are great for personalizing the space. Patchwork panels incorporating favourite motifs such as underwater creatures, jungle animals or letters always look striking. Attach them to the wall with fabric ties, loops or eyelets (grommets). Plain calico fabric pockets can be customized, too, with felt letters spelling out your child's name, or photocopied and transferred images of the contents (see pages 86–7).

Foam cube furniture is a good idea for toddlers right up to ten-year-olds. Simple shapes can be moved around the room and re-covered when they get wrecked, as they undoubtedly will be. You can easily

make the furniture yourself. Source some fire-retardant foam and make up a fabric cover, loose or fitted, in your chosen colour. Sew some pockets on each side to act as book holders.

Window seats are ideal in bay and square windows, combining storage and seating. Slimline foam cushions can be anchored or laid loosely on the top and covered with interesting fabrics. Chunky round bolsters placed at each end make good temporary pillows and give visual punctuation to the space.

ABOVE Children always prefer a large floor cushion, or a beanbag, to conventional seating, since it allows them to sprawl on the floor without restriction and in comfort.

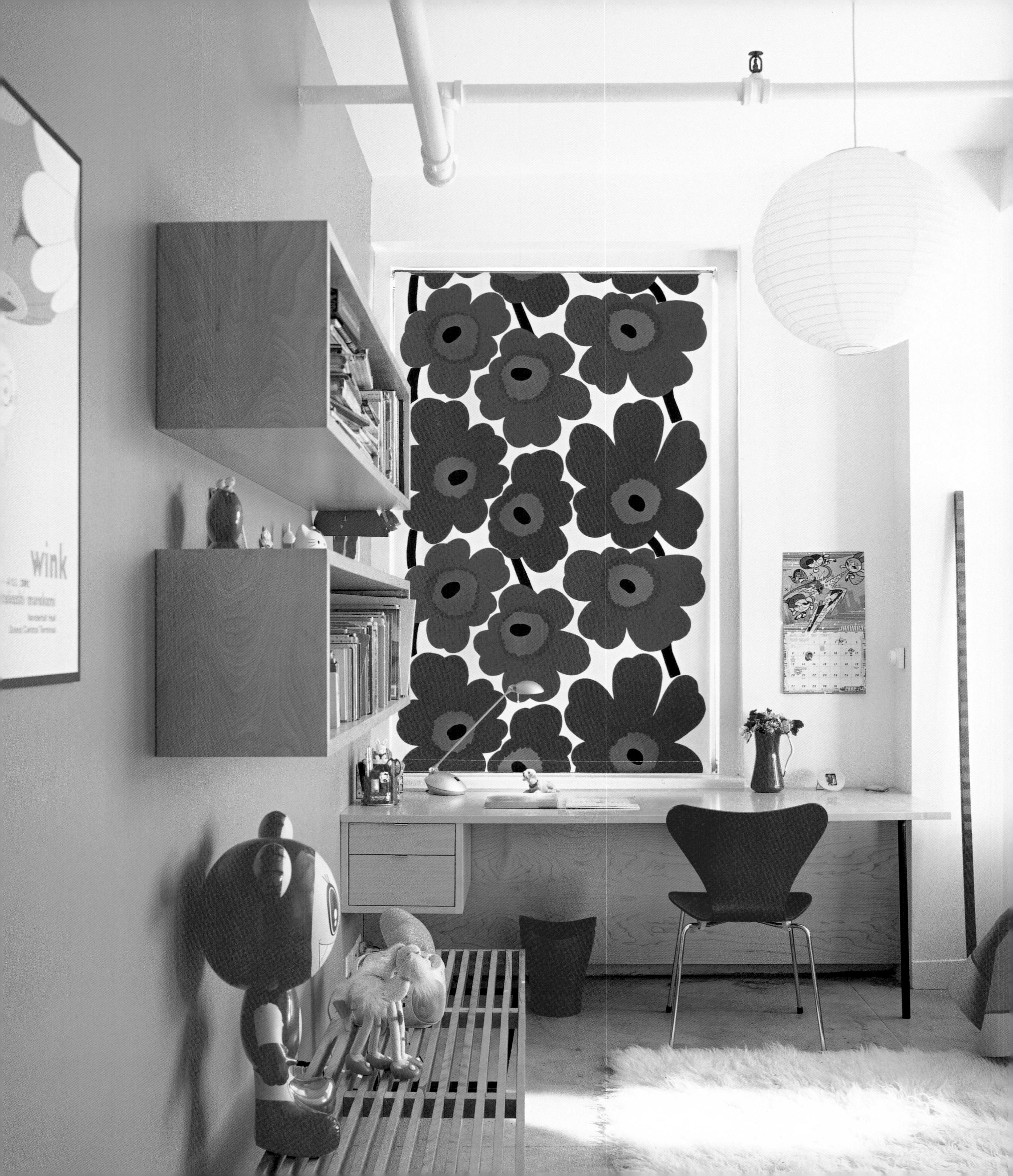
wink

WINDOW TREATMENTS

Curtains and blinds in simple checks and stripes can be trimmed with white bobbles, glittery beading or thick stripes for decorative effect in a pared-down space. For an older child's room, choose fabrics printed with words or numbers for roller or Roman blinds, if you want to educate by stealth. Pelmets with pointed edging trimmed with tassels or buttons are neat and graphic, while a wooden pelmet can be painted the same colour as the wall behind it so that it blends into the background. Floor-length curtains are only a good idea if you choose a fabric that will not age with your child, although you can reuse a large

quantity of fabric for making floor cushions or blinds for the next offspring. Make sure that you fix the curtain rail or pole securely to the wall as children will undoubtedly pull on the curtains.

The windows themselves provide opportunities for decoration in children's rooms. Different colours of cellophane fixed to multi-paned windows create a stained-glass effect (see also page 102), and strings of glass beads attached firmly to a window frame create pleasing light reflections. Older children may appreciate wooden Venetian blinds, roller blinds with small shapes cut out or plain curtains that they can customize in some way.

attention. Replace any out-of-date curtains with a brightly coloured roller blind or a Roman blind, and think about buying a new rug.

Changing the backdrop against which all the furniture is placed is a good way of altering the space. Switching from neutral walls to a dramatic colour or vice versa will have enormous impact. If your child can't decide which is her favourite colour this week, try painting one wall in a dramatic shade, or even in a textured finish such as metallic paint or half blackboard and half magnetic for an individual look.

If you once bought matching furniture for your child's room that now looks dated, think about painting each individual piece. Older children like to see different-coloured drawers in a chest of drawers, so enlist their help in creating a multicoloured scheme that they can implement with you. Alternatively, paint everything white and place all the toys in see-through containers. Nursery furniture decorated with motifs can be sanded down, painted over and given a final coat of matt varnish to suit an older child.

There are various stages in a child's life, such as when a baby becomes a toddler, when you may decide to buy a new bed. This is often the catalyst for redecorating a child's room. The bed can provide a new focus for the room. Painting the frame and buying or making new bedlinen, adding a new bed cover or installing a bed that is metal-framed rather than wood and hanging a muslin or other fabric canopy above the bed will shift the style of the room and give it a more grown-up feel. Sleigh beds are available in bare wood and MDF, which you can then paint.

ABOVE Adding cork tiles to a plain wall provides a large, versatile pinboard for artwork, certificates and wall charts. Provided that the tiles are not pre-finished, paint them the same colour as the wall or a contrasting colour. Devoting a whole wall to display in this way is a good idea for older children as they accumulate sporting achievements and collectable mementoes.

EASY MAKEOVERS

If a child's room has not been decorated for a while and is starting to look tired, there are a few easy makeovers that will freshen up the space.

Just by changing the bedlinen and curtains you can make an enormous difference. For crisp accessories, decorate some storage boxes in a matching fabric, add a new lampshade or make up bright labels that go with the bedlinen. Rejuvenate beanbags with a different fabric and a new filling, as this will compact with age. Animal prints, a plain fake fur or textured cotton plus appliquéd motifs will all attract a child's

RIGHT Changing the paint colour, adding new drawer pulls and attaching rope handles to under-bed storage are easy makeover solutions for furniture that needs livening up. An instant bed canopy can be formed by draping and suspending muslin.

SPACE EXPLORER'S BEDROOM

Outer space is a popular and inspiring subject for any

imaginative child, girl or boy. When it comes to creating a

themed bedroom, a galaxy of planets, rockets and meteors

in a range of colours and textures is hard to resist. This

contemporary night-sky room is stimulating by day and

soothing by night, thanks to ingenious special effects such

as glow-in-the-dark paint and glitter 'space dust'.

ABOVE To Infinity and beyond. Individual planets and spaceships were created by painting on pre-traced outlines with water-based emulsion (latex) paint in different colours.

Gus, aged six, is the proud inhabitant of this space-themed room, which is the envy of all his friends. Such a popular theme should endure for several years and take Gus up to the pre-teen stage. If he tires of the decoration sooner, it will be relatively easy to paint over the walls and adapt the existing fixed storage to suit a different style.

Decorator Nikola Ward was given more or less free rein by Gus's mother, Rachel, when she commissioned Nikola to design an 'Outer Space' bedroom. Nikola's first major decision was to paint the ceiling a deep blue to resemble the night sky. She then re-created the earth's rim in one corner of the room. To make it seem more realistic, she ran a semi-circle of glitter paint around the edge. Glow-in-the-dark paint was used for the detailing on the planets, spaceships and meteors to create a night-sky look.

LEFT A desk in the centre of the bedroom, with a noticeboard that doubles as a shelf behind, is reminiscent of mission control, with its bird's eye view of the galaxy and a full spectrum of stationery for compiling flight reports. A space-pod lamp is a fitting addition to the bedside table.

Using colours from a range of space paints specially manufactured for children's rooms, Nikola painted on the planets, alien spacecraft, rockets and meteors by hand in matt emulsion, after tracing pictures and space shapes from books, enlarging them and then outlining them on the wall.

Similar effects could be achieved by making or buying stencils, although it always looks more effective if you add in the smaller details by hand. These particular alien spacecraft appear to be in permanent orbit, travelling at the speed of light around the room, the tiny alien space travellers just visible in their viewing pods.

In any themed room, it can be fun to link in the storage solutions with the story. Here, the bunk beds have been sprayed silver to resemble the high-tech materials associated with space travel, and the

ABOVE Gus surveys outer space while swinging his legs from the top bunk. The bunk beds mean that sleepovers are easy to arrange for Gus's friends, who jump at the chance to spend a night here.

ABOVE Gus catches up on information about the planets. Even his bedlinen continues the space theme and complements the night-sky ceiling perfectly.

RIGHT Highly practical cupboards have been turned into a very appealing decorative feature in this storage corner. Disguised as lockers, they have been labelled with the names of famous astronauts, making finding clothes each morning an exciting adventure for Gus.

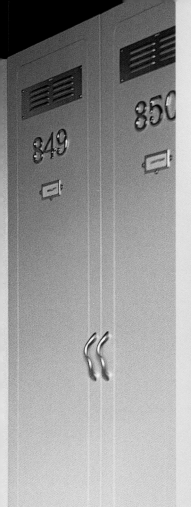

wardrobes have been elevated from otherwise ordinary contemporary cupboards to personalized space lockers. These were tailor-made from MDF, with each cupboard defined with a routed and curved groove. The finishing touches were provided with plastic air vents sprayed with silver metallic paint, and chrome card holders and door numbers screwed onto the doors. The names of famous astronauts, such as Buzz Aldrin, Buzz Lightyear and, of course, Gus, are written on the name tags. Inside the cupboards there are adjustable clothes rails, which can be heightened as Gus grows older, as well as deep drawers for clothes and toys, and shelves for large board games.

Contemporary furniture suits the outer space theme well. A small-scale desk, incorporating a movable display shelf, and a polypropylene bedside table with lunar-module-style silver legs are a focal point for the room. Accessories, such as pen holders, are hooked into the peg holes of the display shelf, adding to the overall organization. Perched on the table is a bedside lamp that continues the lunar-module look.

A circular, multicoloured rug over the sanded floorboards echoes the moons of Saturn and provides warmth and comfort underfoot. Silver-grey woodwork links in with the silver-framed bed and space lockers, and also continues onto the corner shelving unit beneath the windows. Rachel designed these shelves as a convenient place for her son to store and display large books and frequently used toys. The shelves are made from MDF and fitted with sturdy struts and shelves for heavy items. They are finished off with a curved top and painted the same silver-grey as the woodwork elsewhere in the room.

ILLUMINATED CAROUSEL

This brightly coloured wall light made from felt and fairy lights provides visual interest in a nursery or toddler's room, and also functions as a decorative wall hanging.

Easy to assemble, the carousel can be made up in a variety of colour combinations to suit the decoration of your child's room. The animals could be replaced with clowns and performing seals, forms of transport or musical instruments. Other shapes you could make using the same techniques include a lighthouse, space rocket, woodland fairy tree and an old-fashioned circus. The materials used are easy to obtain: any good artists' suppliers will have sheets of coloured felt and polyboard (for the backing), while fairy lights are widely available from specialist lighting shops and department stores.

MATERIALS AND TOOLS
❖ Pencil ❖ Polyboard ❖ Scalpel (mat knife) ❖ Ruler
❖ Sheets of different-coloured felt ❖ Black pen
❖ Sharp scissors ❖ Fabric/craft glue ❖ Needle and black thread ❖ Fairy lights ❖ Bradawl (awl)
❖ Masking tape

1 With a pencil, draw the outline of the carousel to the desired size on the polyboard and cut out the shape with a scalpel (mat knife), using a ruler as your cutting edge. Draw the outlines of the components of the carousel structure – base, roof and centre – onto the felt with a black pen,

allowing for the shapes to be about 2.5cm (1in) larger on the outside edges than the polyboard outline of the carousel. Cut out with scissors. Wrap the felt around the polyboard, covering the white edges completely, and secure the shapes in position with fabric glue. Leave to dry.

2 Cut out the carousel details – the central vertical pole and small stripes, blue wavy roof border, green base stripe, palm trees and two layers of small circles for the roof detailing – in felt to the required size. Glue into position.

3 Photocopy the templates of the elephant and giraffe (see page 183) to the required size and cut out the shapes. Using the templates, cut out the animals in felt. Create the detailing, such as the eyes, with a needle and black thread, and use different shades of felt for the animal markings and the elephant's toenails. To make the animals look three-dimensional, draw around the cut-out shapes on a different shade of felt, making the outline slightly larger. It's a good idea to draw around the reverse side of the animals, so that you don't mark the side to be displayed. Glue the larger outline onto the back of the original animal shape. Glue a few small pieces of polyboard on to the back of each animal, so that the finished animals are more rigid and stand proud of the carousel. Glue the animals onto the carousel.

Mark the position of each fairy light on the carousel and poke a sharp pencil or bradawl (awl) through each point. Very carefully thread the individual bulbs through each hole from the back of the carousel and secure the flex in place on the back with masking tape. Tape any leftover bulbs to the back of the carousel.

ABOVE The 3-D quality of the animals has been achieved by giving the shapes an outline in a different colour and gluing small pieces of polyboard to the back.

FLEECE BLANKET

This colourful fleece blanket includes useful side pockets of various sizes for storing a favourite bedtime book, flashlight and teddy bear.

Making your own child's fleece blanket allows you to choose colours that fit in with the room's scheme: the horizontal stripes can be multicoloured, as here, or simply two-colour for a more sophisticated look. The finished blanket provides a soft, welcoming surface on which to sit during the day, as well as giving an extra layer of warmth at bedtime.

MATERIALS AND TOOLS

❀ Tape measure ❀ Fleece fabric in purple, blue, orange, red and pink ❀ 2 metal clamps, available from builders' merchants ❀ Scissors ❀ Pins and sewing needle ❀ Sewing machine and thread ❀ Embroidery thread and crewel needle

1 Measure the length of fabric required from one side of the bed to the other. Here, each stripe measured 45cm/18in; an additional 4m (4⅓yd) was needed for the single backing colour. If the bed sits up against a wall, you need measure only from the bottom of the mattress on one side to 7.5cm (3in) above the floor on the other side. Add on the size of the pockets, as well as 5cm (2in) to each side and 1cm (½in) on either end for the seams.

To ensure that you cut the fleece in a straight line, place each colour, in turn, along a table edge at the point where you wish to cut and clamp the fabric to the table. Rest the scissors along the edge of the table as you cut. Trim the top of the fleece, to ensure a perfect right angle.

2 Once you have cut out all the required stripes in different colours following the above method, pin them with right sides together and machine-sew, taking 1cm (½in) seams.

3 To make the pockets, cut out the fleece in the desired colour and to the required size, allowing an extra 1cm (½in) for the seams. Turn under the edges on three sides of the pocket and pin in place. Using embroidery thread in a contrasting colour, blanket stitch the top edge. Sew the pockets in position with running stitch.

4 For the blanket lining, cut out a piece of fleece that measures the same as the finished blanket, plus 1cm (½in) all round for the seams. With right sides together, stitch the striped side to the backing, taking a 1cm (½in) seam and leaving a gap of about 45cm (18in) on the side edge that has no blanket pockets. Turn the blanket right side out through the gap and finish the sewing by hand with slip stitch.

PAINTED PLATES

Children, as well as adults, will have enormous fun creating their own painted plate designs, which they can then hang proudly on the wall or display on the mantelpiece.

A mini children's party industry has evolved around the simple process of decorating china, even though it is very easy to do at home with specialist water-based ceramic paints. For the best results, follow the paint manufacturer's instructions carefully and have your oven set at the right temperature. However, as oven temperatures can vary, you may need to experiment a few times before creating your masterpiece. Although the paints are non-toxic and the plates will be dishwasher-proof, it's a good idea not to use them every day because the paint may eventually wear off. All the basic techniques used for painting plates are included in the instructions given here for the crocodile plate. Once you and your child have practised a few of them, you can go on to produce any number of designs.

TOP Once the basic shapes and background colour have been applied using a reverse stencil technique followed by simple brushwork, the details are added with a ceramic paint pen.

ABOVE Painting the rim in a contrasting colour and scratching off decorative details with a cotton bud is simple to do but effective.

MATERIALS AND TOOLS
❋ Glazed white plate ❋ White spirit (mineral spirits) or hot, soapy water ❋ Sticky-backed plastic (masking film) ❋ Soft pencil ❋ Scissors ❋ Sponge, cut into small pieces ❋ Specialist water-based ceramic paints ❋ Ceramic tile or plate (to use as a palette) ❋ Pin ❋ Cotton buds (swabs) ❋ Black ceramic paint pen ❋ Paintbrush ❋ Oven ❋ Kitchen paper (for wiping brushes and mopping up spills)

1 Clean the plate thoroughly with white spirit (mineral spirits) or hot, soapy water, to remove any grease. Transfer the desired shape (see the templates for the crocodile and foliage, crab and shells, fish or tiddlers on page 181) onto the sticky-backed plastic (masking film) with a pencil. Cut the designs out with scissors. Peel off the backing paper and stick the designs onto the centre of the plate.

USEFUL TIPS

Before starting work, make sure that you have all the materials to hand, and cover the table with a waterproof cloth. Then the fun can begin, with a minimum of fuss or mess.

2 With a piece of sponge, dab yellow ceramic paint around and over the edges of the designs. This is known as a reverse stencil technique and can be used for any simple or recurring shape you may want to apply. Use a ceramic tile or plate as a palette for all your paints.

3 Before the paint is completely dry, remove the designs with a pin. Clean away any paint that has leaked beneath the plastic with a cotton bud (swab). Allow the paint to dry.

4 Define the edges with a soft pencil and then trace over them with a black ceramic paint pen. Leave to dry. These pens can also be used to provide fine detailing, such as eyes, dots and geometric shapes.

5 With a paint brush or cotton bud, carefully fill in the crocodile shape with green ceramic paint.

6 Using a piece of sponge, dab blue paint around the rim of the plate. While the paint is still wet, use a cotton bud to create the white 'waves'. This technique is useful for creating simple white patterns or geometric designs.

Leave the plate to dry for at least 24 hours. When completely dry, put the plate in a cold oven and set the temperature at 150° C (300° F, gas mark 2). When the temperature is reached, allow to bake for 35 minutes. Turn off the oven and allow the plate to cool in the oven. Once dry and fired in an oven, the ceramic paint should be dishwasher-proof, as long as you have followed the manufacturer's instructions.

125

FAIRY MURAL

A mural enlivens any child's room, and this pink fairy mural will, no doubt, delight almost every little girl, while a painted footballer will probably appeal more to a boy.

'Any colour as long as it's pink' is a mantra that few parents with daughters between the ages of three and seven will escape entirely. Satisfy your child's obsession, without having to redecorate the whole bedroom when the passion diminishes, by painting a large mural in one corner.

Refer to the template on page 182 for the fairy shape, which shows how to build up the design in stages. Unless you are creating a tiny fairy, you will need to draw the outline freehand with a hard pencil, using a series of circles. Glitter, beads and small mirrors simply add to the girliness of this gorgeous creation. You could also use magnetic paint. Painting it on before the pink, say, of the fairy's dress will mean that you can add mirrors with magnetic backs and other magnetic shapes and move them around to change the pattern of the dress.

MATERIALS AND TOOLS

❁ Water-based emulsion (latex) paint in mauve, white, bright pink, flesh pink, yellow, gold and blue ❁ Wallpaper paste ❁ 10cm (4in) paintbrush (for background) ❁ 2.5cm (1in) brush (for filling in) ❁ Square brush, flat brush and lining brush (for detailing) ❁ Hard pencil ❁ Pinky-white pearlescent wash ❁ Pink and lilac iridescent glitter ❁ Coloured felt pens for detailing the nose, eyes and freckles ❁ Soft cloth ❁ Sheets of pink and lilac neoprene ❁ Plywood star shapes ❁ Silver metallic spray paint ❁ Silver glitter ❁ Fast-tack glue ❁ Sparkly pipe cleaners ❁ Small decorative mirrors, beads and sequins

LEFT Dressing up as a fairy, complete with flouncy pink skirt, wings and a wand, is a little girl's idea of heaven.

RIGHT A wall fairy is a source of wonder in a small child's bedroom, especially when the light fades and the mirrors on the dress twinkle gently.

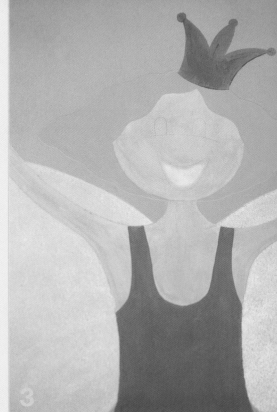

1 Make up a colourwash with a 50/50 mix of mauve paint and wallpaper paste and apply to the wall in random directions with a 10cm (4in) brush to achieve a mottled finish. Allow to dry, then draw the outline of the fairy on the wall in pencil. Fill in the fairy shape with white emulsion (latex) paint applied with the 2.5cm (1in) brush.

2 With the 2.5cm (1in) brush, paint the wings with the pearlescent wash and, while still wet, blow on the iridescent glitter. (This can be quite messy to do, so cover up any furniture and the floor.) Paint the dress shape bright pink and leave to dry. Then paint the face, body, arms and legs flesh pink.

3 Paint the hair yellow. Draw on the crown and shoes, and paint them gold. Draw on the eyes, nose, mouth and freckles with a pencil, then cover over the lines with a felt pen. Paint the mouth white, but wipe the colour back with a damp cloth so that it looks soft and not lurid.

5 Spray the wooden stars with silver and, while still wet, sprinkle silver glitter over them. Stick the stars to the wall using fast-tack glue. (Bear in mind that when you come to remove the stars, the glue may damage the wall surface.)

4 For the background stars, which complete the 3-D effect, cut out various sizes of star from the neoprene, using the pre-formed plywood stars as a template. (These materials are available from craft shops.) Stipple the pearlescent wash over the neoprene sheets and, while still wet, sprinkle iridescent glitter over them.

6 Finish off the eyes by dabbing on blue paint with a soft, damp cloth. Bend and twist the sparkly pipe cleaners, also available from craft shops, into shape for the wand. Glue the wand into position. For the flowers on the dress, draw on the outlines using a pencil and then paint them yellow. Glue on decorative mirrors for the centres of the flowers. Embellish the crown, dress and shoes with sparkling accessories, such as beads and sequins.

ABOVE The finished fairy looks set to dance off the wall thanks to 3-D accessories and reflective surfaces. For a boy, you might choose an outer space theme instead (see pages 114–17) or a footballer in his full kit, with a shiny football.

organic living

WHAT IS ORGANIC LIVING?

An organic approach to the home has far-reaching benefits, especially where children are concerned. Introducing the next generation to the advantages of living simply and well, while developing an easy sympathy for nature, regular recycling habits and an affinity for authentic materials, reinforces the importance of conservation and children's respect for the environment.

The organic ethos means appreciating the value of materials over convenience, and quiet order over technology overload, as well as encouraging a less hectic pace of life. Using natural materials such as organic paints for decorating reduces the risk of children developing allergies and asthma, and recycling furniture and fabrics where possible makes economic sense. Parents are naturally concerned about food additives and genetically modified crops, so these days many children are introduced to organic food at a very early age.

Such a pure approach does not have to mean less choice when it comes to living well – organic food, fabrics, paints and recycling methods are now readily available. In fact, children instinctively appreciate the pleasures of recycling, creating various playthings from all manner of discarded materials. The traditional cycle of growing, consuming and re-using is once again establishing itself, so it is likely that subsequent generations will have an eye on the organic as well as on the technological.

RIGHT Perfect symmetry, together with sleeping space for four children, is achieved in a rustic home by placing bunk beds on either side of the door. Each has storage underneath. Natural colours are used throughout, with the wooden panelling painted with a subtle, pale blue colourwash.

ABOVE Natural linen sheets and pillowcases are decorated with appliquéd panels of black-and-white *toile de Jouy* motifs to provide a touch of luxury in a painted and recycled traditional metal cot (crib). Use organic paints when recycling junk furniture, and remember that young babies should not sleep on pillows.

OPPOSITE In a converted industrial building where the living space has been recycled from an old factory, this platform playspace has been assembled from wooden crates and pallets, with insertions of painted plywood panels. The entire platform is clearly visible from a communal office, so that the work and play spaces are permanently connected.

HOW TO ACHIEVE IT

Think twice before you buy anything new. Look around for second-hand furniture and renovate it yourself – it's amazing what a lick of paint can do – and recycle it for any children you may have later. But don't hold onto things that you know deep down you will never use again; provided they are in good condition, donate any unwanted belongings to your local charity shop. Make recycled storage by painting up fruit trays and crates, or using tea chests sanded smooth, tin cans stripped of their labels and wooden planks laid on building bricks for an instant bookshelf. (Paint the bricks to prevent brick dust from rubbing off onto the shelves.) As part of a weekly routine involve your children in your efforts to recycle newspapers, glass and cans.

When it comes to toys, there is nothing more appealing to a young child than a large cardboard box – many a brand new electronic toy has been discarded in favour of its packaging. Cardboard boxes with wheels attached with brass fasteners, empty drink cans transformed into turbo-charged pullalong trucks and, of course, the enduring rickety go-cart are all great favourites. In fact, even a plain undecorated cardboard box will provide hours of imaginative play.

Making new objects from shiny packing materials, bubblewrap, egg boxes and juice cartons unleashes a natural creativity that seems to diminish when adulthood approaches. In addition, all sorts of discarded materials can be used for educational as wekk as fun activities, such as constructing forts, castles, dolls' houses and rockets.

Developing an appreciation of nature is another activity that children are instinctively drawn to. Watching small creatures, observing the changing of the seasons, playing outdoors and finding pleasure in growing plants and flowers are all ways of encouraging children to become involved with nature.

ORGANIC DECORATING

Using natural materials for decorating and furnishing a child's bedroom or playroom offers a certain level of versatility and quiet sophistication that differs from the usual riot of loud colour more often associated with junior rooms. It also allows the children's artwork and other colourful treasures to stand out.

The smooth and soothing tones of pure wood, the quiet colours of a neutral palette and the rich textural variations of pure cotton, linen and canvas hemp provoke a calm and relaxed atmosphere. Stone, terracotta and wood all age gracefully in the home and withstand the knocks imposed by children in a more dignified manner than chipboard, Formica and nylon carpet. Sometimes convenience and economy are worth overriding for a reassuring organic feel. Dust mites can cause allergies to worsen in children as well as adults, so avoid clutter, carpets and heavy furnishing fabrics in favour of easy-to-dust clean lines.

Although modern decorating and cleaning materials are convenient and may work out less expensive than their organic counterparts, their toxic properties are not as commonly known. Many people assume that non-toxic paints are available only in dark, earthy colours, but new production techniques and experimentation with natural pigments have resulted in an even wider range of tones.

Organic paints differ from conventionally manufactured ones in several ways. Their natural ingredients, such as citrus oils, linseed and chalk, allow a wall to 'breathe', so dust particles don't bounce off the sealed, painted surface and into the atmosphere. This porosity does mean, though, that the paint takes longer to dry than a conventional one, and it marks more easily. A protective layer of water-based matt varnish will provide a wipeable surface, which is particularly important in children's spaces.

Organic paints cost a little more and have a shorter lifespan than non-organic ones, but if cheaper paints trigger your child's asthma, for example, convenience and economy pale into insignificance. Solvent-based paints are harmful, both to health and to the environment. Gloss, shellac and eggshell are the worst offenders because they often cause chestiness, headaches and asthma for those with an acute sensitivity. If you cannot avoid using these kinds of paint, try the less toxic alternatives such as organic and water-based shellac and topcoats. Look out for the VOC (volatile organic compound) ratings, which are a standard measurement of solvent levels in paint. These range from minimal (0–0.29 per cent), low (0.3–7.99 per cent) and medium (8–24.99 per cent) to high (25–50 per cent) and very high (more than 50 per cent). There are also environmental considerations to take into account: conventional paint often creates a 90 per cent wastage in the manufacturing process – far more than in organic processes.

These days, all the main types of paint are lead-free, apart from a few radiator paints – check the can if you're in any doubt. However, if you're stripping off paint that is more than a few decades' old in a child's room, be aware that you may be exposing yourself (and the atmosphere) to dangerous traces of lead. Always wear a mask and ventilate the area as much as possible. If you're pregnant, leave paint-stripping to someone else. The most toxic conventional paints are generally those used for woodwork – doors, skirtings (baseboards) and furniture. Pure organic decorators shun solvent-based paints altogether by leaving skirtings and doors untreated and simply coating them with beeswax.

Many organic paints behave in a slightly different way on the brush from conventional paints, so it's a good idea to experiment with testers on all the

surfaces you wish to cover before embarking on any major redecoration. Organic paints lend themselves well to subtle, loosely applied colourwashes that are less scrupulously smart than planes of matt colour, and more in keeping with a free, natural approach. Gentle tones of pebble, slate, fern or violet have a dreamy quality that fuses well with wooden furniture and toys and natural, textured fabrics.

Once you've considered how organic you want to be with your paint and have finished decorating, it's a good idea to allow the space to dry out completely for a few days before you install furniture and allow your child to sleep in the room. Finish off your decorative efforts with a ribbon of fairy lights at picture-rail height to give a soft glow and calming influence to the space.

ABOVE Recycled furniture can be smart as well as eco-friendly, especially when painted in natural colours and organic paints. Matting, in the form of seagrass and sisal, is a good natural flooring solution.

OPPOSITE Recycling wood to make new children's furniture fosters a sense of eco-awareness in a generation that will need to know about its importance in society. Combining wood and neutral colours is, in any case, a smart decorating choice.

ORGANIC FABRICS

Children and natural fabrics have a pleasing affinity for one another. Wrapping a newborn baby in a woollen shawl, covering a child's bed with a handmade cotton quilt made from scraps of baby clothing, and hanging nubbly linen at a window all make great comforters in a child's space.

Even though cotton is considered a natural fabric, as a crop it has often been treated with harsh chemicals. Organic cotton, however, is grown without using them and it is also left unbleached. This makes it especially suitable for baby clothing, and many suppliers have sprung up during the last few years. It can also be used to make sleep pillows (see pages 150–1). Some organic cotton is bleached, but without using chlorine, which is itself a hazardous product. Even non-organic cotton feels a lot better on the skin than synthetic fabrics because it allows moisture to evaporate. It's also a good choice for furnishing fabrics as it washes and dyes well.

While linen is often considered too expensive for a child's room, one delicate pillow or floor cushion is a real treat and will demand respect. Linen takes much less time to grow than cotton and is, therefore, not treated so heavily with pesticides. It washes well, lasts a long time and is luxurious to the touch. It is naturally elegant and also works well as a sophisticated window treatment or bed throw.

Wool is sometimes dyed with harsh chemical dyes, but on the whole it is a safe and versatile material for clothes, blankets and toys. Fleece, whether as clothing or as a bed blanket, has become a firm favourite in many children's rooms, and every child adores the comfort it offers. However, few people realize that this reassuringly warm fabric is often made from recycled plastic bottles, offering a pleasing link between comfort and conservation.

ABOVE Improvise a high chair by making a padded cushion insert for an existing wooden seat. It blends into a tablescape far better than any plastic shop-bought model designed for the same purpose.

On chilly nights, the welcome warmth of a hand-knitted hot water bottle cover is a personalized way of contributing to a good night's sleep (see pages 152–3). Knitted cotton is just as comfortable as wool, but an added advantage of wool is that it comes in a lot more colours. Organic wool is available from specialist suppliers (see page 186).

Once rejected as an outdated 1970s wall covering, hessian (burlap) has resurfaced as a decorating material. Its tough, rough texture adds visual interest and its natural brown tones reinforce a neutral scheme.

Lambskins are often used to line cots (cribs) and Moses baskets. Their soft, warm texture is thought to have natural healing properties, which is why lambskins are often used for premature babies to lie on. Organic versions are tanned naturally with mimosa extracts and are free from chemical residues. These lambskins are washable, too, and make good playmats for older babies and toddlers, as well as warm liners for pushchairs (strollers) and buggies.

Beanbags covered with natural hemp, leather, nubbly linen and thick cotton twill have a natural smartness. Filled with recycled polystyrene beads, they provide a neat organic twist in a child's space. Raffia-seated chairs have a rustic edge and they wear well, while wooden chairs can be softened with tie-on calico cushions.

Cushions covered with rough hessian, raffia braiding and combinations of linen, canvas, fake fur and cotton fleece create visual interest and physical comfort in a child's space. Mixing materials and natural colours is the classic way of creating a pure and organic decorative scheme. It is a handy coincidence that neutral, natural colours possess their own elegance. Cool oatmeal tones, rich earthy browns, and taupes and soft whites combine to look smart, clean and appealing in any space.

LEFT A compiliation of cosy woollen throws, soft cotton and linen sheets, fleecy soft toys and generous cushions is carefully lit with a string of delicate fairy lights suspended on the wall. Soft muslin panels hung from the ceiling create a cocooned space.

RIGHT In this low-level shared bedroom where storage is built under and in between the beds, pets bring nature indoors and enjoy the light, airy and uncluttered environment.

OPPOSITE Animal mania is at large in this playroom where walls and fabrics merge. Giant sleeping lions on the walls are accompanied by soft sheepskin rugs and leopard-print beanbags on the floor.

APPRECIATING NATURE

Bringing the natural world into children's spaces is an obvious way of encouraging young people to develop an appreciation of living things.

Houseplants have long been ignored as tools for living, and yet they serve as important natural air purifiers. Bamboo palms, rubber plants, humble chrysanthemums and gerberas, together with philodendrons, all absorb harmful chemicals such as benzene, which is found in unpainted MDF (medium-density fibreboard), plywood and other composite boards. Formaldehyde is another hidden pollutant absorbed by many plants. It is most commonly found in cavity wall insulation, furnishing fabrics, stain repellent on carpets and non-iron clothing, as well as furniture made from MDF and heavily varnished pieces.

Growing seedlings from scratch before transplanting them into the garden is fascinating for children and gives them a daily checking routine. An avocado stone pierced with cocktail sticks and rested on the rim of a glass jar, tomato plant seeds, mustard and cress and nasturtium seeds will all grow rapidly. A windowsill and a wooden tray are all you need to get started. An old fruit crate or a simple sturdy cardboard box will make good organic seed trays for beginner gardeners.

Playing outdoors often results in children bringing all sorts of wildlife into the home. Glass jars filled with leaves and twigs make good temporary dwellings for found insects such as wood lice, caterpillars and spiders. Keep them for a few days before releasing them back into the 'wild'.

Children adore making pictures and still lifes from seashells, pieces of tree bark, broken branches and twigs, preserved leaves and nuts. A simple flower press can be used for flowers and leaves. Stars can be made from thick pieces of dark twigs tied together with jute string, providing a quick lesson in geometry at the same time. Older children will enjoy stripping the bark from fallen branches with a penknife and making mock wigwams and campfires with their booty.

THE GOOD LIFE

It's a mistake to think that living the organic life means that you have to make design or style compromises. In the north Italian countryside, Katrin and her husband, Omero, have converted an old, abandoned windmill. Inhabited by nesting birds when they first discovered it, the windmill is now an eco-aware home, complete with a children's clothes and furniture design business. Their home displays all the good things about an organic approach to interior design: simplicity, comfortable minimalism and a concern for healthy, eco-living.

LEFT The Advent envelopes are made from baker's bread bags and stamped with small numbers, one for each day of Christmas. Each bag contains a small gift, such as a handmade angel, small chocolate or game.

LEFT Cool white walls and woodwork and a tiled floor evoke a pure and simple ethos that is softened with wooden furniture for comfort and a woodburning stove for warmth. An arched window frames the view of the river.

OPPOSITE One of the early products that Katrin designed was this pull-along horse made from discarded wooden scaffolding. Wherever Laura is playing, she loves to have it nearby.

When Katrin and Omero first saw the romantic but dilapidated windmill four years ago, it had been long abandoned, the sails had already been removed and birds were nesting wherever they could indoors. The couple then embarked on an extensive renovation project, establishing their home in the top two floors of the windmill and later converting the ground floor into a large workshop.

When Katrin gave birth to their daughter, Laura, a year later, she decided to launch a business from home that could grow alongside her baby. Starting out by making one-off children's clothes from recycled linen and selling them to exclusive stores and by mail order, she then turned her thoughts to furniture. She commissioned several carpenters to make cribs, cots and beds to her own designs using recycled wood that included discarded wooden builder's scaffolding

and old wine barrels. Katrin liked the idea of taking very simple materials and re-using them in new contexts. When used as builder's scaffolding, the wood is unprepossessing but Katrin gives it a new lease of life by recycling it into desirable, simple, clean-lined objects, such as a chunky crib on rockers and a simple kitchen table.

Once Katrin had started to recycle linen and other natural fabrics into exquisitely simple designs for baby clothes, she included in her repertoire pull-along toys and a babywalker made of recycled wood. They are undeniably more charming than standard plastic examples of the same things.

Both sides of the business have continued to grow and develop, and Katrin now employs three carpenters and three seamstresses. Her furniture lines and superb children's clothes are sold in stores all over Italy and as far afield as New York and California.

ABOVE This delightful baby's crib was one of Katrin's first furniture designs. It is made from wood that has been recycled from old wine barrels.

RIGHT A full-sized eco-chic cot made from recycled wooden scaffolding has a satisfyingly robust design. Pure cotton sheets and a linen throw make up the organic bedlinen.

RIGHT An organic version of a traditional Japanese futon, this chunky bed base sports wide planks, sunken spaces for bedside lights and two head supports, and there is plenty of room for a king-size mattress.

ABOVE Star cookies, made with organic ingredients, are always a favourite when guests come to visit. They bake well in the woodburning stove, which doubles as a heating source.

LEFT The wooden trestle table, as well as the simple wooden dressers and storage cupboards, were all made to Katrin's own designs.

the home. Nowadays it heats just the kitchen, while other woodburning stoves around the home provide heat for the remaining rooms.

Recycling is an important part of the family's life. Encouraged by her own beliefs and a willingness to pass on an eco-awareness to her child, Katrin has created a thriving business that allows her to work from home and bring up Laura in the calm of the countryside. But escaping from work is not quite so easy when your home is also your place of work and there is a constant stream of visitors to the workshop. Nevertheless, living and working in the same building does have obvious advantages. The main one is that Katrin is able to pop in on her daughter at key times during the working day, which she enjoys very much. In addition, when she returns home after business trips abroad, visiting stores and looking for inspiration, there is much less disruption to family life.

BELOW Laura was introduced to organic living at a young age. She loves helping her mother, an accomplished cook, in the kitchen, cutting out the cookie shapes.

The windmill's interior has been painted white throughout for a clean, cool atmosphere tempered only by natural wood and neutral linens. In the bedroom, the focal point is a giant futon-style bed base, which Katrin designed. Placed near the window, it allows views out over the local landscape. When Laura was a baby, she shared the bedroom with her parents, sleeping in a cot also designed by her mother.

In the kitchen, simple wooden freestanding furniture houses all the cooking paraphernalia. Katrin has designed tall dressers to hold the everyday china and glasses, while rustic larder cupboards contain all the less visually appealing items. Her chunky table doubles as a worksurface for making homemade bread and cookies, and is conveniently placed close to the woodburning stove. When the family first moved in, this stove was the only source of heat for

RECYCLED TOY KITCHEN

Pretend baking and household chores are much more fun in an integrated kitchen that a child has helped create from an old cardboard box.

Children often get more pleasure from playing with the packaging of their toys than with the contents, so why not recycle a sturdy old cardboard box to create a portable kitchen? This simple design incorporates a four-ring hob with heat controls, washing machine, fridge/storage cupboard, as well as storage for the knives and forks, cooking utensils and oven gloves. There are many variations on this theme, including a workbench with toy tools and a small shop. All you need is some imagination and a willing child to come up with all sorts of suggestions to create a special toy that will be played with time and time again.

Turn the box upside down and strengthen all the bottom edges with black gaffer tape. Strengthen the remaining edges, which now form the top of the box, with grey gaffer tape, and run a length of tape across the middle, too, to reinforce the join. Paint the top of the box with grey emulsion (latex) paint.

For the burners: Turn four paper plates upside down and paint their edges with grey emulsion paint. Leave to dry, then paint their centres with black emulsion paint. Secure the plates in position with double-sided tape around the inside edges. Use epoxy resin to attach four flat chrome door knobs for the controls in the centre. Embellish them with two orange circular stickers cut into different shapes.

For the washing machine door: Using a compass and pencil, draw two large circles, approximately 7.5cm (3in) apart, on one side of the box. Cut out the outer circle with a craft knife, then cut around the inner circle to make a ring. Paint the ring with grey emulsion paint. Once it is dry, re-attach the ring using several layers of black gaffer tape fixed to the inside of the box, to form a hinge. Stick on a sheet of opaque acetate with double-sided tape to the inside of the ring, to make the window in the door. Attach one of the

MATERIALS AND TOOLS

✢ Sturdy cardboard box ✢ Gaffer tape in black and grey ✢ Water-based emulsion (latex) paint in grey and black ✢ 4 paper plates ✢ Double-sided tape ✢ Epoxy resin ✢ 4 flat chrome door knobs (recycled or new) ✢ Orange circular stickers ✢ Compass and pencil ✢ Craft knife ✢ Tough, opaque acetate ✢ Pair of kitchen door handles and fittings (recycled or new) ✢ Thin-ridged, black corrugated card ✢ Bradawl (awl) ✢ Metal pegboard hooks, 2.5cm (1in) long ✢ Plastic cutlery basket ✢ Cooking utensils

kitchen door handles to the ring using metal screws and nuts. For the control panel, fix on three square corrugated card panels with double-sided tape. Use orange circle stickers to make the controls.

For the fridge/store cupboard: On the opposite side of the box, use a craft knife to score three sides of a rectangle, 4cm (1½in) in from the edges of the box, to make the door. Make sure that you score just enough for the flap that you create to open and close easily. Screw on the other kitchen door handle to the door. For the detailing, add a strip of corrugated card 7.5cm (3in) deep to the top edge of the door.

For the storage: On the remaining two sides of the box, make two holes with a bradawl (awl), using the metal pegboard hooks as a positioning guide. Slot the hooks snugly into the holes for hanging the cutlery drawer and utensils.

SCENTED SLEEP PILLOW

Filled with wheat and lavender, these animal-shaped sleep pillows will release calming vapours to help lull tired children to sleep.

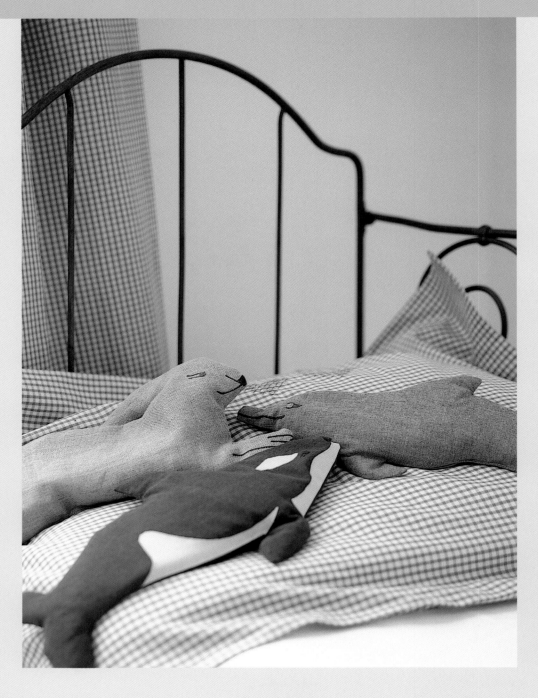

Warming these pillows in a microwave or an oven will increase the intensity of the scent, but you will need to make them from closely woven, 100 per cent cotton fabric – preferably organic cotton. Wheat is used because it retains heat while allowing the lavender to permeate the air. These bags are unlikely to affect children who suffer from a wheat allergy, but if you are at all concerned, seek advice from your doctor. Put the pillows in a microwave for two minutes or in an oven heated to 180° C (350° F, gas mark 4) for ten minutes.

A template for the whale is given on page 183. There are all sorts of other simple shapes you could draw yourself, such as a rabbit or dolphin, as illustrated here, or a frog, hen, even a small dog.

MATERIALS AND TOOLS

❉ Scissors ❉ 60 x 40cm (24 x 16in) of dark blue 100 per cent cotton fabric ❉ 3 small pieces of white or cream calico (bleached or unbleached muslin) ❉ Iron-on fabric adhesive ❉ White and blue thread and needle ❉ Sewing machine ❉ Blue embroidery thread and crewel needle ❉ 650g (23oz) wheat (available from animal feed suppliers or health stores) ❉ 2 tablespoons fresh lavender

1 Make paper templates for the whale shape and markings. (Photocopy the templates on page 183 to the desired size or sketch them yourself.) With scissors, cut out two whale shapes in dark blue cotton and three markings in calico (muslin), according to the templates. Cut out the iron-on fabric adhesive in the same shapes as the markings but slightly smaller.

2 Position the white markings on the whale's body and insert the iron-on fabric in between the two pieces of fabric. Iron the markings to firm them into position. For a neat finish, machine- or hand-sew around the white patches. This will also position them more securely.

3 Machine-sew the white shapes with white sewing thread onto the whale. Embroider the eye with light blue embroidery thread. Pin the two blue pieces of fabric right sides together. Hand-sew together with blue sewing thread, with a 1cm (½in) seam allowance, starting at the tail end of the belly and leaving a 10cm (4in) opening. For extra strength, stitch the pieces together twice. Clip all the corners, to make the inside less bulky, and turn right side out. Press. Fill with wheat and lavender. Machine-sew the opening.

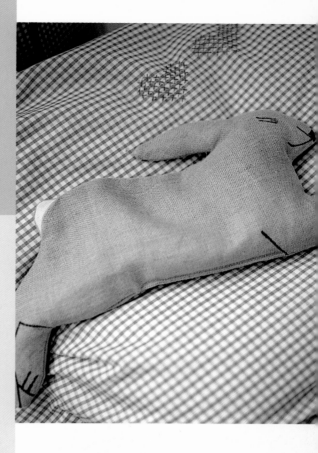

ABOVE Children of all ages love animal-shaped pillows. This wholesome rabbit has been made with closely woven natural linen and brought to life with embroidered detailing and a calico bobtail.

HOT WATER BOTTLE COVER

What can be more comforting for a tired and shivery child than to snuggle up to a hot water bottle covered in the softest knitted cotton?

This hot water bottle cover is simple to make for anyone who knows how to knit. Fasten it together with buttons or, if it is for a child under three years old, attach a strip of Velcro to each of the open ends. For a completely organic feel, you could use unbleached wool, which is available from specialist organic fabric suppliers. Either knit your own miniature soft toy to slot into the pocket, or buy one.

MATERIALS AND TOOLS

❋ 1 pair 4mm (no 8) knitting needles ❋ 2 x 50g (3½oz) balls of double knitting cotton, or wool in colour A ❋ 2 x 50g (3½oz) balls of double knitting cotton or wool in colour B ❋ Stitch holder ❋ Small amount of contrast wool for the pocket ❋ 3 buttons or strip of Velcro

ABBREVIATIONS USED

Alt = alternate	St st = stocking stitch
Dec = decreas(e)ing	St(s) = stitch(es)
K = knit	Tog = together
P = purl	YF = yarn forward
Rem = remain(ing)	RS = right side

POCKET LINING

Cast on 19 sts colour A. Work in st st for 8cm (3in), ending with a p row. Leave the sts on a holder.

FRONT

Cast on 39 sts colour A.

1st row K1, P1 to end K1.

2nd row P1, K1 to end P1.

3rd row (button hole row) K1, P1, YF, K2 tog, rib 14, YF K2 tog, rib 14, YF K2 tog, rib 2.

4th row continue in rib.

5th row continue in rib.

Continue in st st, increasing 1 st at each end of next 3 alt rows, to give 45 sts.

Next row, change to colour B.

To work stripes, knit 4 rows in each colour.

Work 12cm (4¾in).

Place pocket

Next row (RS) K13.

Change to pocket colour, K19.

K13 sts in main colour.

Keeping stripes correct, continue in st st until work measures 20cm (8in), ending with a p row.

Next row: K13, slip next 19 sts onto a holder and, in their place, knit across 19 sts of pocket lining.

Knit to end. Continue in st st to 28cm (11in), ending with a p row.

Shape top

Dec 1 st at each end of next 3 alt rows, to give 39 sts.

Cast off 5 sts at beg of next 2 rows. 29 st.

Dec 1 st at each end of next 3 alt rows. 23 st.

Work 2 rows.

Cast off 1 st at each end of next 3 alt rows, to give 17 sts.

P1 row. Cast off 17 sts.

BACK

Cast on 39 sts.

Work in st st to match the front without rib and without pocket.

MAKE UP

Press both pieces lightly.

For the pocket top slip 19 sts from the holder onto the needle. Rejoin yarn with RS facing. Work for 2cm (¾in) in rib. Cast off.

Slip stitch pocket top and lining into place. Join back to front, leaving lower edge open. Sew on buttons or fix on Velcro.

outdoor space

CHILDREN AND GARDENS

Gardens and children are made for one another. When children are small, space is often in short supply within the home, so the garden is an obvious place for them to play. As well as using up your children's energy, outdoor playtime also gives you some peace and quiet indoors. The smallest of gardens can be adapted to provide a child-friendly area, while in a larger garden there is space to create a self-contained play zone, which is more like an outdoor room. Ponds are best avoided before children are able to swim, and make sure that any new raised paved or patio area includes curved edging, which is kinder to tumbling limbs than sharp right-angled lines.

Adapting the garden so that, weather permitting, it becomes an outdoor room and an extension of, perhaps, the kitchen, dining area or living room, is an excellent way of bringing the outdoors in and creating a sense of space. Awnings, arbours or glass-roofed gazebos provide some protection from the weather without the expense of building a conservatory or garden room. Outdoor eating areas are perfect for children, especially during the summer when friends can swell lunchtimes into mass catering events. Children can help with the preparations by setting the table and making place names, for example, which all adds to the sense of occasion. For a smaller gathering, arrange finger food on a rug on the ground. And since the excitement all takes place away from the house, the whole process is much more relaxed for parents.

Gardens offer great potential for education, creativity and discovery, too. Watching the seasons change, monitoring the growth of seedlings and plants, and finding new insects under flowerpots are all part of the fun of outdoor living. Setting aside an area as a children's garden is possible in even the tiniest of

courtyard gardens. It can be as small as a miniature garden in a fruit crate (see pages 176–9) or as lavish as a purpose-made potager, complete with scarecrow, wooden signs and a picket fence surround. Whatever the size, children love to have their own space in which they can grow and care for plants, even if it's only a good excuse to shovel some soil into a bucket and pick out the worms!

ALL-SEASON PLAY

Summer is obviously the preferred time of year for being outdoors, but children seem to be blissfully unaware of unpleasant weather and will often want to play outside in all temperatures, rain or shine. As long as they wrap up warm and remove all wet and dirty clothing before they enter the house again, much fun can be had from sloshing around in puddles, creating mud pies and playing in the snow.

Creating an outdoor space in which children can play throughout the year is a good way of easing congestion in the house and offers a pleasant change of scenery for them. It also gives them the opportunity to get out of a centrally heated house and breathe in some fresh air.

Play zones that incorporate slides, swings, climbing ropes, play platforms and decking make great adventure areas. Many manufacturers supply versatile systems that can be adapted to fit your space and budget, although, again, it's possible to design and build your own. Toddlers need lower platforms and slides than older children, so a degree of flexibility is important if you are designing your own system.

LEFT A disused garden shed has been slightly modified with wooden shutters held up on chains and double doors to create a stripey playhouse where half the neighbourhood can indulge in a serious game of shops.

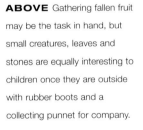

ABOVE Gathering fallen fruit may be the task in hand, but small creatures, leaves and stones are equally interesting to children once they are outside with rubber boots and a collecting punnet for company.

Toddlers as well as older children adore climbing, and a climbing frame, particularly in a limited space, is a godsend. Freestanding swings are also a good idea in a small garden; simple versions suspended from trees or wooden frames are the most economical with space. They are available in metal or wood, but it can be fun to design and build your own

Safety is obviously very important in the garden. National safety organizations provide useful guidelines for buying and using outdoor play equipment. Manufacturers also provide safety information about where to site large pieces of equipment in the garden. Before building any equipment of your own, make sure

ABOVE In a large informal garden a small pond has been given over to the children, whose play shed fits snugly alongside a slide and rope swing that merge well into the fruit trees. The overall effect is one of a relaxed family garden rather than a purpose-made children's area.

that the finished article will conform to safety regulations and that you're happy that the materials you have chosen are sturdy enough for the purpose.

Making dens is one of the memorable parts of childhood, and often the simpler the construction, the better. Large branches and leaves woven into a wigwam shape around the base of a tree trunk and finished off with a purpose-made skull-and-crossbones flag or colourful bunting are often all that's needed.

Decking lends itself well to gardens where children like to play. Edged with picket fencing and a gate, it creates a comforting (and safe) enclosure for babies and toddlers, while forming a clean barrier between the house and wet or muddy grassed areas. Raised seating areas can be incorporated into the decking, as can low-level planters for children's easy-to-grow flowers or plant pots containing herbs. It is often a good place to allow the children to do messy painting or play sessions, where spills are easily mopped up.

Freestanding trampolines are perennial favourites in larger gardens. Round or rectangular, they are weatherproof and provide instant entertainment as soon as the weather switches from wet to dry. In a decked or paved area, it is possible to install them at ground level, although this means excavating below and making a permanent feature of the trampoline.

EXCLUSIVE CHILDREN'S AREAS

Dedicating a specific space for children to use gives them exclusive access to their own 'secret' garden and a great sense of freedom that is often lacking in today's over-protective society. By providing some basic play equipment and setting out the area in zones of activity you can encourage your children to garden, play and learn all at the same time.

In a small garden, create a separate play area by dividing off a space with picket fencing or willow or bamboo screening. Alternatively, plant a fast-growing hedge such as privet or laurel. A small playhouse, swing, wooden structure or climbing frame may be the focus of the area, but then you can incorporate special elements such as a small water feature, a raised miniature flower bed or a child-sized seating area.

Furniture is important in a children's area. Small wooden twig benches and chairs, miniature picnic tables and painted wicker seats are all charming additions to an outdoor room, and sturdy, too. Small benches can double as basic obstacle courses when hooked onto low-level climbing frame steps and can be used as medal podiums for sporting endeavours. Your children will probably enjoy helping you paint,

stain and varnish outdoor furniture. Improvised seating looks good: sawn-off tree trunks topped with hardwood planks or zinc panels make interesting variations on the traditional wooden bench.

If you cannot afford miniature versions of the classic chairs, you can achieve a similar elegance by building a round tree seat to encircle an established tree. Hammocks are popular with children, as well as adults, and come in many different fabrics, styles and sizes. Make sure that they're held securely in position, and always supervise children younger than three.

Look around your garden and see whether any existing elements lend themselves to being transformed into a child-friendly area. Just one 'climbing tree' is often all that's needed to fuel young imaginations. Similarly, a climbing rope or rope ladder offers plenty of scope for trainee pirates, spies and gang leaders. Make sure that homemade rope ladders or climbing ropes are very securely attached to their supports and check them regularly for signs of wear.

Accessories for a children's play area include wind chimes, which make good outdoor projects for older children to make when they are feeling creative, scarecrows, painted wooden lanterns and bird houses.

ABOVE Delightful stepping stones made from metal daisies form a random floral pattern on a plain lawn.

CENTRE A raised open summer-house provides a large deck to carry adult-sized seating, benches and hammock, which offer a watchful view over a trampoline and pleasingly coordinated seesaw. Trampolines provide hours and hours of dry-weather entertainment for children of five and over. They never seem to tire of the novelty of catapulting themselves into the air.

RIGHT Pre-teen ten-year-olds crave time away from their parents in much the same way as true teenagers, so individual hammocks and twirling tree banners are the ideal solution for mending sulky moods.

PLAYHOUSES AND TREEHOUSES

You will probably experience as much nostalgic pleasure from helping re-create a miniature world in the form of a playhouse or treehouse as your children will in playing in it. A playhouse can be as simple as a garden shed embellished with floral or gingham curtains and a window box, or as grand as a purpose-made children's house, complete with painted exterior, thatched roof and mock chimney. A treehouse, on the other hand, could be a child's play shed raised up on stilts to create an air of detached elegance, with a pulley system installed to transport anything from soil and sand to containers full of water or even snacks.

A simple, inexpensive playhouse can be embellished with interesting detailing. Enliven a plain roof by sticking on loose shingle, woven willow, or bamboo or thatched panels. Custom-made pargeting (patterned plasterwork) painted in one or more colours, a name plate and door number, shutters and wooden window boxes all make versatile features that children will love to help decorate. Playhouse manufacturers will often custom-make accessories or build a house to a specific architectural specification to match your own house.

Playhouses and treehouses offer a great way of involving the children in some form of decorating, and because both structures are outdoors, you can be much more relaxed about any mess that's created as a result. The interior always looks complete when fitted out with simple curtains – muslin, faded florals and gingham all serve the purpose well. A painted floor that matches the walls and ceilings will make even a small shed feel bigger, and miniature furniture rather than a full-sized table or bench will obviously fit the space better. If you feel inclined, you can make choosing the exterior and interior paint colours into a learning experience for your children.

There are a number of different themes you can adopt. A literary theme could be inspired by Winnie the Pooh books and include a roughly hewn and misspelled wooden sign for a Hundred Acre Wood atmosphere. A seaside theme can be created by painting a playhouse in two-colour vertical stripes and finishing it off with multicoloured bunting, outside and in, and wooden steps and balustrades painted in ice-cream colours. A rustic log cabin look is best created with unpainted wood and filled with chunky wooden furniture, a stripy rug and garden relics such as discarded branches and an old lantern.

Accessorize these small homes with wheelbarrows, beanbags, weathervanes, ships' lifesaving rings and flags. A welcome mat is a good grown-up touch. Inside you can be as sophisticated as you like. A small glass jar of flowers from the garden, a neat collection of books and comics, together with the essential den kit of binoculars for spying and birdwatching and, of course, a pretend kitchen, are probably all that's required for a play space that will be used over and over again. Young children will simply enjoy transporting their pushalong toys in and out of the space. A small bell hung at the entrance is a fun way of letting them announce their arrival.

A sandpit is a good extension of a playhouse or play area and provides hours of entertainment for toddlers and older siblings. It can also be bought as a freestanding piece that sits on the patio or grass, or can be built into an area of decking or paving. Make sure that you always cover it at night to keep animals and garden debris out of the sand.

A treehouse built on stilts offers an additional play area underneath, which can be used as a sandpit or even a secret HQ. Hang canvas from underneath the house and attach it with large eyelets (grommets) and rope or camouflage netting.

OUTDOOR PLAY

Children love to play outdoors, especially when the weather is good. In even the smallest of gardens, adults and children can happily co-exist. Decorative screens are a neat solution for separating a play area from an adult seating space, and brick-built barbecues can be screened from view with trelliswork or metal arbours and double up as an outdoor storage area for push and ride toys. Miniature picnic tables and garden seats are readily available and look good in their own child-centred space, perhaps next to a herb bed.

Playing outside can be as simple as a single child riding a tricycle or as inventive as a group of children staging an outdoor theatre production, complete with stage, costumes and props. Many indoor games can seem more fun and allow for a greater degree of creativity when transferred outside. Painting and drawing benefit from the extra space as well as the natural flotsam and jetsam that may be added to collages and drawings for a 3-D effect. Dressing-up and role-play are made more adventurous when there are secret hiding places, trees and paved areas in which to act out different roles.

Musical chairs can become musical shapes: cut out some star, cloud or tree shapes from sturdy paper or card for the children to stand on and take a portable stereo outside. To set the scene for an outdoor party, string some bunting from the trees (see pages 174–5) or, if the gathering is in the early evening, fix up some outdoor lights or lanterns.

Certain elements in the garden may be adapted for the purpose of playing. A brick-built barbecue makes a good impromptu puppet stage, a couple of wheelbarrows become buses for toys and chariots for a quick race across the lawn, and pergolas are transformed into grand entranceways for imaginary castles and homes.

Games that involve tearing around on bicycles, pogo sticks, scooters, Rollerblades and in miniature vehicles are the simplest form of getting exercise and producing tired children. You will need to think about where to store these frequently used items. A lockable garden shed, garage, utility room or porch is the easiest to access, while a wooden chest will accommodate smaller playthings. Bicycles and helmets can be fixed to garage or shed walls with sturdy hooks, while a collection of footballs, tennis balls and basketballs can be kept in a net suspended from the wall or ceiling, alongside sports rackets.

BALL GAMES

Sport can be accommodated quite easily in a garden, whatever its size. In a courtyard garden, create a play wall with a marked target, against which balls can be kicked. A basketball hoop, fixed directly onto an outside wall, is a simple but effective way of encouraging ball skills and of passing the time on a dry day – a healthy alternative to the computer and television. Make sure that they're not placed too close to any windows, though. A tennis practice swingball is indispensable for active older children. Freestanding nets for badminton, volleyball or soccer are good investments, if you have enough space. Cricket, rounders or baseball are popular at large family gatherings, as are boules and croquet.

TRADITIONAL GAMES

Games such as hopscotch, draughts (checkers) or snakes and ladders can be painted directly onto a patio, deck or other hard surface as a permanent feature. For smaller numbers, a simple game of piggy in the middle, catch or throwing a frisbee is always popular. Building obstacle courses also fires children's imaginations. Use blankets, wooden planks, individual

ABOVE A small verandah offers a cosy and sheltered place for a quick game of draughts (checkers). You could go one step further and paint a chequerboard directly onto the wooden decking, creating a permanent feature.

building bricks and outdoor furniture to create a mini-maze of endurance. It makes a good challenge for the adults, too, once the children have finished the construction and set up a time trial!

Hunting for clues that lead to treasure, such as sweets or a small toy, chocolate coins or seasonal treats such as Easter eggs, is always a crowd pleaser, especially at children's parties or family gatherings. (Keep pets out of the way, though, while you hide the treasure.) Older children, in particular, enjoy making their own treasure maps and clues, so enlist their help.

SLEEPING UNDER THE STARS

During the summer months, it's a real treat for children to be able to sleep outside, whether in a tent, playhouse or treehouse. For many children this offers them their first experience of camping but in familiar and safe surroundings. Pick a night when the moon is bright and the weather warm. It is usually a good idea for an adult to sleep nearby, just in case of a sudden onset of fear of the dark, spiders in the tent or nocturnal animal noises.

PEACE AND QUIET

Setting up a quiet reading or drawing area provides a novelty location that will also help lure children into the garden and away from their games consoles or the television. Have a small bookcase on castors and some pots of pens and paper in a playhouse or gazebo near the house. This will provide a quiet retreat for them after they have exhausted themselves romping around the garden with friends.

RIGHT Camping outdoors is an adventure that children enjoy much as if it were a trip to the moon. Even though this rather grand 'tent' has all the comforts of home, the novelty of being outside can still become overwhelming if an adult is not close by.

ABOVE Natural walkways can be formed from willow frames laced with fast-climbing plants, from quick-growing bamboo or from plants trained over metal arches until they form a semi-solid awning.

GREEN FINGERS

Creating a self-sufficient garden may seem like a time-consuming pipe dream, yet it doesn't take a great deal of work to set up a small potager, and your children can help. In a small garden, create an area where children can grow their own plants in pots.

Personalize a potager by making items to put in it with your child. Scarecrows are easy and economical to make: thin banners of kitchen foil tied together with natural raffia or jute string form the most basic bird-scarers, while a fully fledged scarecrow is more of a creative endeavour. Use old dressing-up clothes and

hats, stuff a body, arms and legs with old newspaper or straw, and suspend the results on a bamboo stick or wooden pole. Screen off the children's patch with a willow or coppiced-hazel archway, planted either side with a low hedge, or create a gravel path edging to denote the change of area.

VEGETABLES

Fast-growing vegetables include courgettes (zucchini) and other squash, garlic, tomatoes, lettuce and runner beans, which look stunning once they start to wind themselves around bamboo canes and produce chunky green pods. Potatoes, too, are easy to grow, as are onions and shallots. Herbs in pots or planted out in a neat bed produce speedy and pleasing results. Easy starter herbs include parsley, thyme, chives, mint and rosemary.

FLOWERS

Children often need instant results to keep their interest in any project alive, so it's no use planting tree seedlings and asking them to wait five years for a sapling. Instead, plant a mixture of bedding plants that are about to flower, spring bulbs that will return year on year and fast-growing flowers such as pansies, sunflowers, nasturtiums, marigolds and wallflowers. They provide instant colour and a real sense of achievement, without the need for too much daily care. Bunnies' ears (*Stachys byzantina*) are perennial favourites as their soft grey-green leaves really are as soft as rabbits' ears.

SAFE PLANTING

Children are naturally curious, so it's best to avoid planting known poisonous or spiky plants while your children are small enough to pick, touch and swallow anything that looks interesting. As soon as they are old

enough to take heed, make sure that they are aware they should never eat anything growing in the garden. Be especially aware of plants that may be edible but that can also be deadly, such as mushrooms.

If you're in doubt about the toxicity of any of your plants, check at your local garden centre. Flowers that are deadly if eaten include foxgloves (*Digitalis*), monkshood (*Aconitum*), tobacco plant (*Nicotiana*), hemlock (*Conium maculatum*) and laburnum. Although not particularly toxic, some popular garden plants may still cause a severe allergic reaction if eaten or touched, such as aquilegia, lobelia, lily of the valley, daffodil, wisteria, euphorbia and juniper. Spiky plants that can cause skin reactions or simply nasty scratches include cacti, yuccas and roses. They're best avoided in areas of the garden where children are at their most boisterous.

Make sure that your children are injected regularly against tetanus, and if they do have a severe reaction to anything eaten by mistake in the garden, try to take a sample of the plant along with you to an accident and emergency unit.

ENCOURAGING WILDLIFE

Plant butterfly-loving flowers like buddleia, also known as the butterfly bush, which is a pretty and fast-growing shrub. Ladybirds (ladybugs) are children's favourites, and they are useful, too, because they devour a number of pests, such as aphids, that threaten to eat young plants.

A small, shallow pond is ideal for attracting frogs, toads, pondskaters and dragonflies. Never leave small children unattended by a garden pond, even if it's shallow and no matter for how short a time.

ABOVE Improvised scarecrows can be made from recycled garden materials such as fruit crates, buckets and broken brooms. Make hair from hay and straw. An old hat will add authentic detail.

ABOVE LEFT Child-centred areas of the garden are best planted with flowers and vegetables that give near-instant gratification such as sunflowers and courgettes (zucchini). Grow climbers such as runner beans and sweet peas up wigwams, which always appeal to children.

GARDEN GAMES

Winfried and Heather wanted to create a family garden where the generations could mix or be separate, according to the occasion. With that in mind, they adapted their garden to incorporate a play area for their children, Ella, aged 6, and Leo, aged 4, as well as a place for sitting and eating. This frees up space indoors and, with the sliding glass doors, the inside and outside merge, creating an outdoor room where the children can play and explore, at all times visible from the house.

LEFT Many contemplative hours can be spent playing on a swing. This one forms part of a contemporary wooden arbour, which also incorporates a rope ladder and a decked area for potted plants and trained climbers.

RIGHT Decking next to the house allows the kitchen doors to be flung open in the summer, so that impromptu family meals and informal entertaining can take place with a minimum of effort. It also means that the children can play on their own further down the garden while the adults are still able to keep an eye on them.

Winfried designed and made the contemporary playhouse himself from painted marine plywood. It is a home-from-home for the children. Quirky details include a stable door, a variety of window shapes covered with different forms of shutters, fold-down windowsills for storing plants and groceries when the house doubles up as a shop, and a smart, contemporary colour combination of vivid blue and boudoir pink. There is space inside for a toy kitchen and a clothes airer, as well as a couple of child-sized chairs. The children play in the house so often that Winfried is beginning to wish that he had made it bigger.

A bamboo roof, laid over roofing felt, tones in with bamboo fencing elsewhere in the garden and slopes away from the house in a modern manner – reminiscent more of a prairie homestead than a traditional playhouse.

Next door to the smart and colourful playhouse is the sandpit, an inventive and much-used annexe to the children's pretend home, and another space populated by a complete cast of characters, real and imaginary. Made from a kit that includes a netting cover to protect the space at night from cats and other animals, it is neatly inset into a run of decking so that, from the house, the messy paraphernalia of buckets, spades, plastic diggers and containers is not visible at all when the children have set up a complicated game or a network of sandcastles.

Most children between the ages of three and seven seem to be at the height of their imaginary powers, and it appears that Ella and Leo are no exception. The outdoors stimulates their imaginations the most, and with their modern playhouse and a few props, everyone, including adults, visitors and pets, is entertained for hours. They love to create fantastic scenarios and complicated games of everyday activities, such as making meals, admonishing

RIGHT Many an imaginary cooking game has been acted out in this toy kitchen, glimpsed through the round window of the playhouse. Kitted out with toy appliances, the kitchen fits snugly into a corner of the playhouse.

LEFT A miniature clothes rail is useful not only for pretend games but also for air-drying adult napkins.

naughty soft toys and aping adult behaviour in a charming manner. These games can take up a lot of time, so by creating a dedicated playspace in the garden it has meant that the adults get some peace and quiet while still being able to keep a watchful eye out for over-exuberant climbing games or any sibling rivalry getting out of hand. The children, on the other hand, feel that they have their own domain where they feel safe but their play is undisturbed by adults, which is something of a rarity for today's children.

The children absolutely adore their recently acquired playspace. When friends come to play, all the children disappear into the garden for hours on end, regardless of the weather. The adults are interrupted only when there's an urgent need for food or drink, an invitation to attend a drama production, or an impromptu imaginary game for which there aren't enough participants.

ABOVE The garden has been designed in such a way that the children don't feel inhibited in their play. Leo is able to cycle around his outdoor domain without destroying any plants.

RIGHT When the weather is good, Ella and Leo enjoy building sandcastles. The sandpit is set into the decking, which makes it easy to sweep the area clean after the children have finished playing.

ABOVE An edging of pebbles separates the lawn from the sandpit and adds a decorative border around the play area. Wooden planks form paving strips and are a convenient display area for homegrown plants.

LEFT The sandpit, which has been asembled from a kit, is made from hardwood. The rim is a useful feature that helps to contain the sand.

PROJECT
PARTY BUNTING

Flags made from metallic silver and purple fabric and knotted onto jute rope give a contemporary edge to this easy-to-make and inexpensive party bunting.

This versatile variation of the traditional bunting used for sailing regattas and garden parties allows you to substitute a variety of flags to suit any kind of occasion. Different colours, patterns and fabrics give a completely different feel; shown here are a party set and a Hallowe'en arrangement. How sophisticated you make the flags is entirely up to you. The silver and purple flags have been neatly machine-sewn for a sleek effect, while the Hallowe'en bunting is just roughly torn cotton fabric, for an informal look. In a small garden you will need fewer flags, but position them close together to define the space. In a large area, you can make bigger flags and space them further apart for added drama. Indoors, you can hook them over curtain poles or between doorways. For special occasions, substitute thick gold or silver string for jute. For a rustic atmosphere, use natural or coloured raffia.

MATERIALS AND TOOLS

❋ Paper and pencil ❋ Scissors ❋ 3m (3⅓yd) of 115cm (45in) wide purple fabric ❋ 2½m (2¾yd) of 115cm (45in) wide silver fabric ❋ Thread in purple and silver ❋ Sewing machine ❋ 12m (40ft) jute rope for hanging 40 flags

1 Make a paper template in a kite shape to the desired size for the purple flags. The purple flags shown here measure 43cm (17in) from top to bottom and 15cm (6in) across at the widest point. Using the template, cut out the purple fabric, allowing a 1cm (½in) seam allowance all around. Place the shapes right sides together and machine-sew right around the edges, leaving a gap for turning the fabric right side out.

2 Clip all the corners, to make the inside less bulky, and turn the fabric right side out. Press. Repeat the process for the smaller silver flags, which here are 40cm (16in) from top to bottom and 12cm (4½in) across.

For a 12m (40ft) run of bunting, make up 20 flags in each colour. This should allow a generous amount of rope for tying the bunting to its support at each end. Tie each piece of bunting at approximately 15cm (6in) intervals onto the jute rope with a simple knot. Hang the bunting between trees or bamboo poles in the garden.

ABOVE This Hallowe'en bunting is very simple to make. Torn strands of orange and black fabric are tied onto a long length of jute rope for an impromptu party in the pumpkin patch.

MINIATURE GARDEN

Designing and then maintaining a scaled-down garden in a wooden fruit crate is a fun way for children to learn about planting and growing seeds.

Many keen adult gardeners have fond memories of following their parents around the garden, observing birds and insects, noting how bulbs burst into flower in spring, even helping with the weeding. This project will encourage your own children to take an active interest in gardening. Not only will they learn about how plants grow and that patience is an essential part of the process, but they will also appreciate how a garden can be arranged in different areas.

Before you start the actual planting, draw a rough plan on paper of how the miniature garden might look and what your child might want to grow. Be flexible, though, because a trip to the garden centre may throw up new ideas, and remember to choose plants that will not grow too tall for the container.

Instead of planting up a wooden crate, you could use a garden sieve or a zinc container, available from garden centres. Good seeds to try are mustard, cress, cat grass (*Avena sativa*) or ordinary grass seed, although this is not as lush, and dwarf beans, as well as herbs such as parsley, chives and garlic. Flowers that are always popular with children include violas, pansies, grape hyacinths and bulbs such as dwarf narcissi. You could also include some alpines and small conifers for variety.

As well as choosing the plants, think about the various design elements, such as an archway made of wire, a toy wheelbarrow or a picket fence made of lollipop sticks, and encourage your childen to come up with their own ideas. Lollipop sticks, plain or coloured, can be bought from craft stores.

ABOVE In the shade of an alpine strawberry plant, tiny rabbits outside their hutch bring life to a pet corner in the garden.

LEFT A wheelbarrow, miniature vegetable basket and gardening implements make realistic accessories, bringing a sense of activity to the vegetable patch of garlic and chives. If only real gardens were as easy to maintain as this one!

MATERIALS AND TOOLS

❊ Wooden fruit or vegetable crate ❊ Non-toxic outdoor paint or stain ❊ Sturdy black plastic for lining ❊ Drainage material such as polystyrene, gravel or terracotta crocks ❊ Multi-purpose compost ❊ Pot-grown plants, such as alpine strawberry, box, chives, garlic, viola, *Ilex crenata* (a type of holly) and small conifer ❊ Lollipop sticks ❊ Secateurs (pruning shears) ❊ Craft glue ❊ Thin, green garden wire ❊ Gravel, small pebbles, plastic animals, etc., as required ❊ Seeds such as cat grass, mustard and dwarf beans ❊ Natural moss

1 Source a wooden crate from a local market or garden centre – it needs to be deep enough to hold any pot-grown specimens you may want to plant. Paint or stain the outside of the crate in a colour that will blend in with the garden. Line the crate across the bottom and up the sides with

strong black plastic. Puncture the plastic on the bottom with several small drainage holes. Next, add a layer of drainage material. Polystyrene is best because it's lightweight and porous, but you could also use gravel or terracotta crocks. Fill the crate with compost, leaving a 2.5cm (1in) gap between the compost and the rim.

Roughly lay out all the areas of the garden, such as paths, fences, ponds and arches, according to your plan. Before you fix them into their final position, plant up any pot-grown items.

2 To make the fencing, cut up the lollipop sticks with secateurs (pruning shears), and link them together by gluing on a line of additional sticks horizontally. If you wish to paint the sticks, do this before cutting them up. (You can also use lollipop sticks to make log-cabin-style sheds, garden slides and arbours.)

3 To make the arch, cut some thin garden wire with secateurs and twist two strands together for extra strength, and then form an arch. Position in the compost. Carefully wrap an artificial flower garland or the planted ivy around the wire.

Add in other detailing such as loose gravel or stone pathways, wooden seats, miniature pots, flowerpot saucers containing water and carrot and parsnip tops, even small figures, plastic animals and scarecrows. Once you have completed all the details, dampen the compost slightly and sow any seeds or beans, firming them in gently. As a final touch, insert some natural moss, as used for hanging baskets, down the sides of the crate to hide the black plastic. Keep the planted-up garden in a light but fairly warm position at first, but out of the direct sun. Remember to water it regularly.

LEFT AND ABOVE This fairy-theme garden has been designed to fit snugly in a discarded garden sieve and is a smaller, more compact version of the crate garden. A child's collection of seashells is pressed into service as garden ornamentation, with large scallop shells transformed into pools of water and decorated with a colourful medley of smaller shells and pebbles. The plants include grape hyacinths (*Muscari latifolium*), pink *Saxifraga* x *arendsii* and ivy.

FAR LEFT Tiny pebbles mark out pathways and divide up different areas of the garden. Leave plants in their pots while you decide on their final position in the crate.

You may find the following plans and templates useful when you come to making some of the projects. The templates for the painted plates, illuminated carousel and sleep pillow can all be enlarged on a photocopier to the desired size.

MOBILE STORAGE UNIT

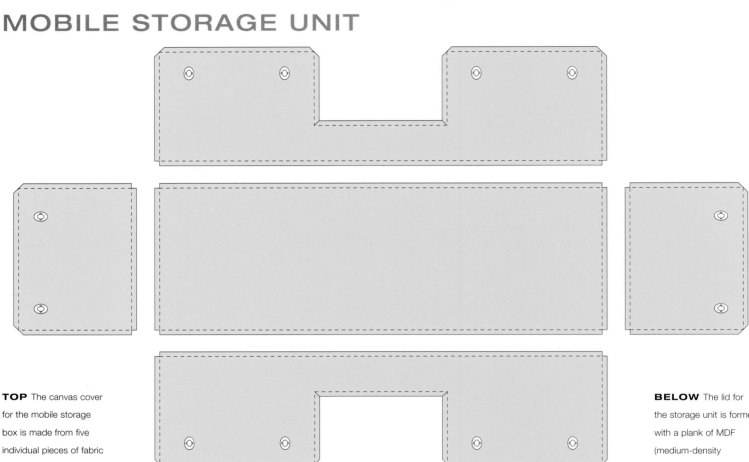

TOP The canvas cover for the mobile storage box is made from five individual pieces of fabric machine-sewn together, providing a sturdy and hardwearing surface. Each side flap is fitted with metal eyelets that form part of a chandler's turn button mechanism.

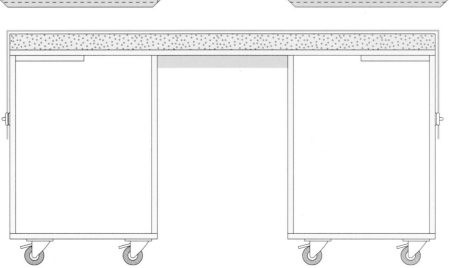

BELOW The lid for the storage unit is formed with a plank of MDF (medium-density fibreboard) that fits across both boxes. Two inner MDF lips measuring half the width of each box are glued and screwed to the underside of the plank. A 7.5cm (3in) thick strip of foam is glued to the top of the plank. Once made up, the canvas cover slots onto the foam-topped lid and is fixed in place with chandler's turn buttons.

PAINTED PLATES

These simple templates can be enlarged or reduced according to the size of your plate. You can use them as a single focal point at the centre of a plate or as a detail around the rim. Children will enjoy providing additional small details and painting each motif in a variety of colours. Ceramic pens are useful for drawing facial features, adding scales to the fish and doing any geometric detailing, while the outlines of the basic shape can be drawn in with a strong black line or another bold colour for definition. Once you've used these templates and practised a few times, it is easy enough to devise your own designs. It's also much more satisfying!

FAIRY MURAL

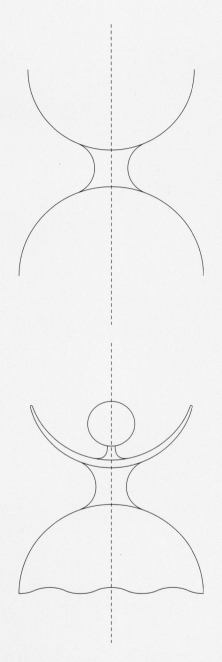

STEP 1 Measure out the wall space you wish to cover with the fairy design. Mark a central vertical line in pencil and use a compass to draw two semi-circles, joined with two smaller ones.

STEP 2 Draw on the head, neck and arm details using a compass, then add the wavy dress hem by hand.

STEP 3 Draw in the legs, hair, crown and wings freehand. Try to make everything as symmetrical as possible.

ILLUMINATED CAROUSEL

These basic animal shapes can be embellished with additional layers of different-coloured felt and stitching. If you prefer to use other animals, simply trace their shapes from a children's animal book.

SCENTED SLEEP PILLOW

This simple whale shape is neatly finished with the addition of three white patches machine-sewn on and finished by hand.

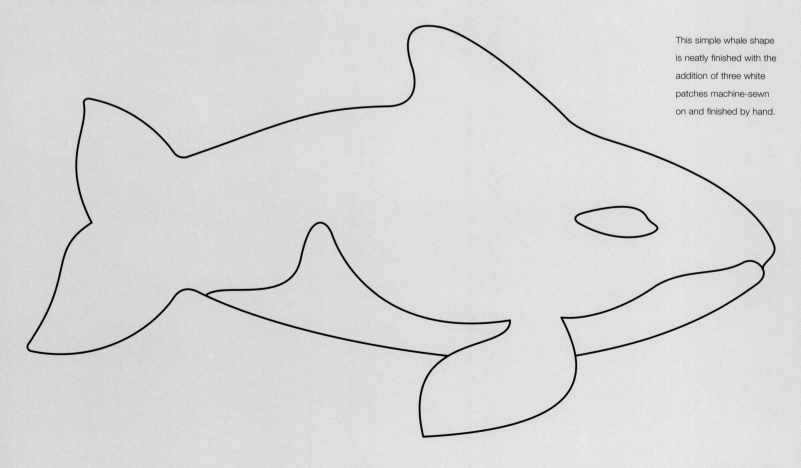

SUPPLIERS

CHILDREN'S FURNITURE

Beau Reve
Call 01923 499467 for details
www.beaureve.com
Themed children's furniture

The Children's Furniture Company
020 7737 7303
www.thechildrensfurniture
company.com
Furniture that grows with
your child

The Conran Shop
81 Fulham Road
London SW3 6RD
020 7930 8309
www.conran.com
Children's furniture, toys and
accessories

Daisy and Tom
181 Kings Road
London SW3 5EB
020 7352 5000
www.daisyandtom.com
Furniture, clothing and toys

Flexa Furniture
1 River View
Walnut Tree Close
Guildford
Surrey GU1 4UX
01483 449900
www.flexagb@flexa.dk
Children's pine furniture

Habitat
Call 0845 6010 740 for nearest
store
www.habitat.net
Children's metal bunk beds
and other furniture, bean bags
and lighting

Heal's
Call 020 7636 1666 for nearest
store
www.heals.co.uk
Contemporary children's
furniture, toys and accessories

IKEA
2 Drury Way
North Circular Road
London NW10 OTH
Call 020 8208 5600 for nearest
store
www.ikea.com
Inexpensive children's flatpack
furniture, toys, fabrics and
accessories

Junior Living
293 Fulham Road
London SW10 9PZ
020 7376 5001
www.juniorliving.co.uk
Smart contemporary furniture in
a range of styles for babies and
children up to age 12

Knights & Daisies
The Old Cooperage
Victoria Business Park
Dallow Street
Burton Upon Trent
Staffordshire DE14 2PQ
01283 711 282
www.knightsanddaisies.co.uk
Children's bespoke furniture

Lionwitchwardrobe
Flat 1
13 St German's Place
Blackheath
London SE3 ONN
020 8305 2334
www.lionwitchwardrobe.co.uk
Beautiful one-off pieces of
children's oak furniture

Next Home
Call 0845 600 7000 for nearest
store
www.next.co.uk
Metal bunk beds, bean bags
and children's fabrics

Oreka Kids
8 South Way
Clavering Industrial Estate
London N9 0AB
020 8884 3435
www.orekakids.com
Stylish, multi-functional furniture
designed to last from early
childhood to adult years

Planet Little
Call 020 8946 3320 for nearest
stockists
www.planetlittle.com
Children's furniture

Tim Chapman
Call 020 7249 7000 for details
Children's wooden beds

CHILDREN'S BEDS AND BEDLINEN

Cath Kidston
8 Clarendon Cross
London W11 4AP
020 7221 4000
www.cathkidston.co.uk
Retro print fabrics and bedlinen,
children's clothing, aprons and
other accessories

Couverture
310 Kings Road
London SW3 5UH
020 7795 1200
www.couverture.co.uk
Bedlinen and children's
accessories

Designers Guild Kids
Call 020 7229 1000 for nearest
stockist
Main store:
267–77 Kings Road
London SW3
www.designersguild.com
Fabrics, bedlinen and children's
accessories

John Lewis
Oxford Street
London W1A 1EX
Call 020 7629 7711 for nearest
store
www.johnlewis.co.uk
Large selection of children's
cots, wooden and metal beds

Laura Ashley
27 Bagleys Lane
London SW6 2QA
Call 0870 562 2116 for nearest
store
www.lauraashley.com
Children's bedlinen and fabrics

Lilliput
Call 01463 7126119 for nearest
store
www.lilliput.com
Nursery and bedroom furniture

Next Home
(see under Children's furniture)

The Nursery Window
83 Walton Street
London SW3 2HP
020 7581 3358
www.nurserywindow.co.uk
Wide selection of children's
bedlinen, gifts and furniture

Osborne & Little
304 King's Road
London SW3 5UH
Call 020 7352 1456 for
stockists
www.osbornandlittle.com
Liberty children's furnishings

Stompa Furniture Ltd
The Old Mill House
Dockfield Road
Shipley
West Yorkshire BD17 7AE
Call 01274 596885 for stockists
www.stompa.co.uk
Multi-functional wooden bunk
beds incorporating storage and
work elements for children and
teenagers

The White Company
Call 0870 160 1610
www.thewhiteco.com
Beds and bedlinen, plus
children's accessories

PAINTS

(see also under Organic
suppliers)

B&Q Head Office
Portswood House
1 Hampshire Corporate Park
Chandlers Ford
Eastleigh
Hants SO53 3YX
www.diy.com
Paints designed specifically for
children's rooms

Crown Paints
Call 01254 704951 for advice
and stockists
www.crownpaints.co.uk
Paints designed specifically for
children's rooms

Dulux Paints
Call 01753 550555 for stockists
www.dulux.co.uk
Glow-in-the dark, glitter and
bright colours for themed
children's rooms

Farrow & Ball Limited
Uddens Estate
Wimborne
Dorset BH21 7NL
Call 01202 876141 for mail
order and stockists
www.farrow-ball.co.uk
Traditional paints and colours

MAIL ORDER

Designers Guild Kids
Call 0845 602 1189
(see under Children's beds and
bedlinen)

Found
0800 316 8121
www.foundat.co.uk
Children's toys and accessories
from the UK and beyond

Junior Street
01768 780112
www.juniorstreet.com
Themed children's furniture,
clothing and gifts

Next Home
(see under Children's furniture)

The Nursery Window
Call 01394 460040 for brochure
(see under Children's beds and
bedlinen)

Urchin
www.urchin.co.uk
Nursery products and furniture

Wigwamkids
Unit 44
Bilston Glen Industrial Estate
Dryden Road
Loanhead
Edinburgh EH20 9NZ
0870 902 7500
www.wigwamkids.co.uk
High-quality children's furniture
in a variety of styles, bedlinen
and accessories

ORGANIC SUPPLIERS

Auro Organic Paint Supplies
Unit 2
Pamphillions Farm
Purton End
Debden
Saffron Walden
Essex CB11 3JT
01799 543077
www.auroorganic.co.uk
Organic and hypoallergenic
emulsion and gloss paints,
stains and safe varnish for
furniture, woodwork and toys

Ecos Paints
Unit 34
Heysham Business Park
Middleton Road
Heysham
Lancs LA3 3PP
01524 852371
www.ecos.com
Environmentally friendly,
odourless and solvent-free
paints and varnishes

Green Baby
345 Upper Street
London N1 OPD
020 7226 4345
www.greenbabyco.com
Organic clothing and bedtime
furniture

Green Fibres
99 High Street
Totnes
Devon
01803 868001
www.greenfibres.com
Organic clothing, fabrics, wool
and home accessories

Katrin Arens
Via per i Molini di sotto
24030 Pontida (BG)
Italy
Call/fax 0039035783336 for
stockists and mail order
Organic furniture and children's
clothes designer (see pages
142–7)

Nutshell Natural Paints
PO Box 72
South Brent
Devon TQ10 9YR
01364 73801
www.nutshellpaints.com

Spirit of Nature
www.Spiritofnature.com
Organic children's clothing,
wool, toys and accessories

OUTDOOR LIVING

**The Children's Cottage
Company**
01363 772061
www.play-houses.com
Outdoor playhouses and play
systems in a variety of styles

Holz Toys
0845 130 8697
Wooden miniature kitchens and
play systems

IKEA
(see under Children's furniture)

Outdoor Toys Direct
0800 169 6016
www.outdoortoysdirect.co.uk
Wooden playhouses, wooden
and metal playsets, giant
snakes and ladders games

Rainbow Play Systems
Head Office: Hillier Garden
Centre
London Road
Windlesham
Surrey GU20 6LN
01344 874662
www.rainbowplay.co.uk
Wooden play systems: climbing
frames, picnic tables, sandpits

Touchwood European Ltd
Broom Barn
Church Road
Coney Weston
Bury St Edmunds
Suffolk IP22 2TJ
01263 761717
www.touchwood-european.co.uk
Tree seats, playhouses,
decking, wooden sandpit kits

TP Activity Toys
Severn Road
Stourport on Severn
Worcs DY13 9EX
Call 01299 872800 for stockists
www.tptoys.com
Metal and wooden play systems

HEALTH AND SAFETY

**Royal Society for the
Prevention of Accidents
(ROSPA)**
Edgbaston Park
353 Bristol Road
Birmingham B5 7ST
www.rospa.co.uk
Information about all aspects of
child safety in the home and
garden

INDEX

PICTURE CREDITS

The publisher wishes to thank the following photographers and agencies for their kind permission to reproduce the following photographs:

2–3 Carel Verduin/SANOMA Syndication; 5 Alexander van Berge/Elle Wonen; 6 above Peter Marlow/Magnum; 6 centre Alexander van Berge/Elle Wonen; 7 above Alexander van Berge/Elle Wonen; 7 centre Alexander van Berge/Elle Wonen; 7 below Giulio Oriani/Vega MG; 8 Peter Marlow/Magnum; 11 Alexander van Berge/Elle Wonen; 12–13 Hans Zeegers/SANOMA Syndication; 13 Edina van der Wyck/The Interior Archive (owner: Imogen Chappell); 14–15 Alexander van Berge/Ouders Van Nu; 15 Alexander van Berge/Inter Gamma; 16 Paul Grootes/SANOMA Syndication; 17 Gilles de Chabaneix (stylist: C. Ardouin)/Marie Claire Maison; 18–19 Alexander van Berge/Ouders Van Nu; 19 Verne Fotografie; 20 Verity Welstead/Homes & Gardens/IPC magazines; 21 left Alexander van Berge/Elle Wonen; 21 right Verne Fotografie (Luc Vincent); 22 left & right Alexander van Berge/Ouders Van Nu; 23 left Jeroen van der Spek/SANOMA Syndication; 23 right Otto Polman/SANOMA Syndication; 24 Alexander van Berge/VT Wonen; 25 Hans Zeegers/SANOMA Syndication; 26 Joyce Vloet/ SANOMA Syndication; 27 Reto Guntli/Red Cover; 28 Per Gunnarsson (stylist: Annelie Tongren); 29 Renee Frinking/SANOMA Syndication; 32 Alexander van Berge/Forbo; 33 Alexander van Berge/Elle Wonen; 34–5 Renee Frinking/SANOMA Syndication; 35 above S. Erkelbout (concept & real: C. Soulayrol, creat: C. Vannier)/Marie Claire Idees; 35 below Per Gunnarsson (stylist: Annette Ekjord & Susanne Swegen); 36 Alexander van Berge/VT Wonen; 38 Alexander van Berge/Elle Wonen; 39 Dennis Brandsma/SANOMA Syndication; 40 Giulio Oriani/ Vega MG; 41 Gianni Basso (Casa architetto Massimo Sottili)/Vega MG; 42 E. Barge (real: C. Ardouin, l'architecte Jean MAS realise la conception du gros oeuvre)/Marie Claire Maison; 43 above & below Peter Marlow/Magnum; 44 Paul Grootes/SANOMA Syndication; 46 Winfried Heinze; 60 Alexander van Berge/VT Wonen; 60 above right SANOMA Syndication; 60 below right Verity Welstead/Red Cover; 61 left Dennis Brandsna/SANOMA Syndication; 62 above Hans Zeegers/SANOMA Syndication; 62 below Alexander van Berge/Ouders Van Nu; 63 Alexander van Berge/Elle Wonen; 64 Hotze Eisma/ SANOMA Syndication; 65 Ray Main/Mainstream; 66 Fritz von der Schulenburg/The Interior Archive; 68 Alexander van Berge/Ulrika Lundgren; 69 Erik van Lokven/SANOMA Syndication; 70–1 Alexander van Berge/Elle Wonen; 72 Alexander van Berge/SANOMA Syndication; 73 Alexander van Berge/VT Wonen; 74 left & right Ray Main/ Mainstream; 75 Hotze Eisma/SANOMA Syndication; 76 Camera Press; 77 left Hotze Eisma/SANOMA Syndication; 77 right Ray Main/ Mainstream; 78–9 Giulio Oriani/Vega MG; 85 Alexander van Berge/ Elle Wonen; 92 Alexander van Berge/Elle Wonen; 94 S. Erkelbout (sty: C.Soulayrol, C. Vannier)/Marie Claire Idees; 95 left Alexander van Berge; 95 right Alexander van Berge/Inter Gamma; 96 left Edina van der Wyck (owner: Wright & Teague)/The Interior Archive; 96 right Giulio Oriani/Vega MG; 97 Alexander van Berge/Inter Gamma; 98 Mark Seager/The Picture House (www.wigwamkids.co.uk); 99 John Dummer/SANOMA Syndication; 100 left & right Alexander van Berge/Elle Wonen; 101 Dennis Brandsma/SANOMA Syndication; 102 Edina van der Wyck (Designer: Shari Manyon)/The Interior Archive; 103 Hotze Eisma (stylist: Julia Bird)/Taverne Agency; 104 left Brigitte Kroone/SANOMA Syndication; 104–5 Alexander van Berge/Forbo; 106 Simon Brown/The Interior Archive; 107 left Alexander van Berge/ Ulrika Lundgren; 107 right Alexander van Berge/Ouders Van Nu; 108 above Alexander van Berge/SANOMA Syndication; 108 below Hotze Eisma (stylist: Julia Bird)/Taverne Agency; 109 Alexander van Berge/ SANOMA Syndication; 110 Ray Main/Mainstream; 111 Hotze Eisma (stylist: Julia Bird)/Taverne Agency; 113 Renee Frinking/SANOMA Syndication; 130 Alexander van Berge/Elle Wonen; 132–3 Ken Hayden/Red Cover; 133 C. Dugied (concept & real C. Soulayrol/M. Tasles (creat. I Strutz/Marie Claire Idees; 134 Peter Marlow/Magnum; 136 Hotze Eisma (R. Smit)/Taverne Agency; 137 & 138 Hotze Eisma/ SANOMA Syndication; 138–9 D Freeman (real : C. Scheve)/Marie Claire Maison; 140 Hertz/Fong residence by William Howard for Dwell magazine (David Hertz aia, Syndesis, architect. Furniture designed by Stacey Fong at Syndesis); 141 Alexander van Berge/Ulrika Lundgren-Woon; 142–7 Giulio Oriani (Katrin Arens)/ Vega MG; 155–6 Joss de Groot/SANOMA Syndication; 158 left Jacqui Hurst; 158–9 Marianne Majerus; 159 Marianne Majerus (designer: Rosewarne); 160 above Marianne Majerus; 160 below Marianne Majerus (designers: Jill Billington & Mimi Harris); 161 Marie Claire Maison; 162 left Ray Main/Mainstream; 162 right Jerry Harpur (Simon Fraser. Mr & Mrs Tennant, London); 163 Winfried Heinze; 164 Ray Main/Mainstream/The Children's Cottage Co.; 165 Renee Frinking/ SANOMA Syndication; 166 Ray Main/Mainstream; 167 right Juliette Wade/The Garden Picture Library; 167 above Gilles de Chabaneix (stylist: V & Y Mery)/Marie Claire Idees; 184 Hertz/Fong residence by William Howard for Dwell magazine (David Hertz aia, Syndesis, architect. Furniture designed by Stacey Fong at Syndesis); 186 Mark Seager/The Picture House (www.wigwamkids.co.uk); 192 Giulio Oriani (Katrin Arens)/Vega MG.

Every effort has been made to trace the copyright holders and we apologize in advance for any unintentional omissions, and would be pleased to insert the appropriate acknowledgment in any subsequent publication.

ACKNOWLEDGMENTS

AUTHOR'S ACKNOWLEDGMENTS

Many thanks to Lorraine Dickey, who had the idea for the book in the first place, and to Senior Editor Muna Reyal for putting together such an excellent and professional team: Helen Ridge, editorial wordsmith *par excellence* and the most charming nagger in the business; Alison Fenton, designer and mother extraordinaire, always willing to go that extra mile – or two; and Rachel Davies, the picture researcher with the stylish eye. Thanks for making it fun and pain free.

I would particularly like to thank the talented project makers (see also below) who translated my scribbled ideas into wonderful creations: Sacha Cohen, Karen Fenton, David Coote, Louise Creasey, Isabel de Cordova, Anjie Davison, Carmel Morgan, Cathy Sinker and Mandy Tarrant. My niece Paula York provided the idea for the nursery storage, thanks to the arrival of her twins Martyn and Laura. Photographers Verity Welstead and Winfried Heinze and stylist Cathy Sinker were instrumental in making the projects and case studies look fresh and interesting. Thank you.

Special thanks as always to Brian, who remained stoic and calm throughout – much appreciated.

Thank you, too, to the families who allowed us to photograph their homes and children's rooms: Winfried Heinze and Heather Dodd, Helen and Andrew Fickling, Rachel Robin and Andy Mallett, Mandy and Stuart Tarrant, Katrin Arens and Omero Gasparetti.

The book would not be the same without the willing children who participated in photography: Hannah and Julia Copestick, Ella Gluyas, Isabella Webb, Hannah Fickling, Oliver and Issy Tarrant, Gus and Jack Mallett, Oscar Morgan, Eloise Fenton, Ella and Leo Heinze. Cool, guys.

PUBLISHER'S ACKNOWLEDGMENTS

The publisher would like to thank Alison Wormleighton and Ingrid Lock.

PROJECTS AND PROJECT MAKERS

The following projects were specially made for Conran Octopus:

Nursery clothes rail, recycled toy kitchen: Cathy Sinker

Drawstring bag, artwork tubes: Isabel de Cordova (020 8673 9750)

Mobile storage unit: David Coote (020 8875 0075)

Illuminated carousel, miniature garden: Karen Fenton

Fleece blanket: Mandy Tarrant (01727 852842)

Painted plates: Anjie Davison, Cactus Creative Workshops (01727 868623)

Fairy mural: Sacha Cohen (mail@sachacohen.co.uk)

Scented sleep pillow, party bunting: Louise Creasey (01727 839081)

Hot water bottle cover: Carmel Morgan (01727 852067)